# ELEMENTARY READING

# Related Titles of Interest

**Webbing with Literature: Creating Story Maps with Children's Books, Second Edition**
Karen D'Angelo Bromley
ISBN: 0-205-16975-9; H6975-0

**Helping Students Learn to Write: An Idea Book for K–7 Teachers**
Joyce C. Bumgardner
ISBN: 0-205-17571-6; H7571-6

**Literature-Based Reading Activities**
Hallie Kay Yopp and Ruth Helen Yopp
ISBN: 0-205-16387-4; H6387-8

# ELEMENTARY READING
## Strategies That Work

**BETH G. DAVIS**
*Brandeis University*

**BONNIE LASS**
*Lesley College*

*Allyn and Bacon*
*Boston  London  Toronto  Sydney  Tokyo  Singapore*

Copyright © 1996 by Allyn & Bacon
A Simon & Schuster Company
Needham Heights, Massachusetts 02194

**Library of Congress Cataloging-in-Publication Data**

Davis, Beth.
    Elementary reading : strategies that work / by Beth G. Davis and
Bonnie Lass.
        p.   cm.
    Includes bibliographical references and index.
    ISBN 0-205-15961-3
    1. Reading (Elementary)   2. Education, Elementary—Activity
programs.   I. Lass, Bonnie.   II. Title.
LB1573.D336   1996
372.4044—dc20                                                      95-42255
                                                                      CIP

Printed in the United States of America
10  9  8  7  6  5  4  3  2  1     00  99  98  97  96

*To the Jedster and Zoë*

# Contents

# Preface

Is this a skills year at your school? Or is whole language in style? Are you at the helm of a literature-based curriculum or in charge of a diagnostic-prescriptive special-needs classroom? Or are you a student of reading methods, boggled by the variety of approaches you are learning?

Reading approaches go in and out of fashion, but one thing is certain. We teach reading in many different ways, even in a single classroom. Grouping practices may range from whole-class instruction to ability groups, skill or interest groups, cooperative pairs, or the one student–one teacher style of Reading Recovery. Most classes use combinations of these methods.

The materials used for teaching reading reflect the same variety. Basal readers, predictable stories, Big Books, children's writing, literature, newspapers, magazines, skillbooks, and games are all found in classrooms.

Do good teachers of reading remain eclectic—that is, use whatever works to help their students to improve their reading abilities? We think so. With the arrival of new reading ideas, good reading teachers (1) add to their arsenal of techniques; (2) refresh themselves with the new, yet hold onto the best of the old; and (3) gain another avenue to reach students.

Our reason for writing this book is to help both experienced and novice teachers plan activities for reading skill and strategy practice. The skills and strategies considered in this book are clustered into four sections: (1) Word Identification, (2) Comprehension, (3) Study Skills, and (4) Attitude and Language.

Each of the fifteen chapters follows a similar format. First, the ability considered in a chapter is defined, followed by reasons that students may need practice with it. Then the advice for instruction comes in two forms: (1) briefly explained techniques and (2) games called Activities to Go. We have provided specific suggestions for alternative use of the games, and we are sure that you will find your own applications. An appendix that provides suggestions for teaching test taking rounds out the book.

We hope that direct teaching of the reading and language strategies that students need is at the center of whatever reading approaches you are using at present. We are equally concerned with increasing the enjoyment of students during reading instruction, perpetuating the reading habit, and increasing students' self-esteem. In seeking to work with students holistically, successful reading teachers combine their expertise and enthusiasm with their students' needs and interests.

We would like to thank Mary Sorenson of Stephen Elementary School in Minnesota; Tressa A. Brown of Plainfield Elementary School District in Minnesota; Pam Ryder of the School District of Whitefish Bay in Milwaukee, Wisconsin; and Judith A. Schoenfeld of Fallon Memorial School in Pawtucket, Rhode Island, for their helpful reviews of the manuscript.

# ELEMENTARY READING

# 1

## Sight Vocabulary

### DESCRIBING THE SKILL

Sally, attempting to read "Neanderthal man lived long ago," stumbles over the first word, but reads the rest of the sentence easily. These last four words are a part of Sally's sight vocabulary.

Sight words are those words readers identify instantly. The words have been memorized and one look at a word can bring an immediate verbal response. This is why a sight approach is often referred to as "look-say." Able adult readers identify almost all words by sight. Therefore, a constantly growing sight vocabulary is the ultimate goal of all word identification instruction.

The ability to identify instantly a large number of words is important for success in reading. Even if a phonics approach is used for beginning reading instruction, there are a number of frequently occurring words that may only be learned through memorization because of their irregular spelling (*of, two*) or that need to be learned quickly, usually before the phonic elements are taught (*game, go*).

. The word identification techniques that proficient readers utilize are sight, context, structural analysis, and phonic analysis, in that order. Beginning readers may use a different learning sequence, however, sight words are often taught first since (1) most children who learn to read on their own begin this way and (2) other word identification instruction is facilitated by a student's grasp of a number of sight words.

What are the appropriate words to teach as sight vocabulary? Many of the words students use in their language experience stories as well as the words they'll encounter in Big Books, poems, and other classroom activities are found in the lists of high frequency words which have appeared in the reading literature. Dolch, Fry, Harris-Jacobsen, Johnson, and Kucera-Francis are some authors of these lists. Included here are the Ekwall "Basic Sight Words" and Johns's list for older disabled readers.

*Basic Sight Words*[1]

*Preprimer:*

| | | | | | |
|---|---|---|---|---|---|
| a | play | him | big | then | it |
| did | too | look | get | where | of |
| have | are | run | house | can | three |

---

[1]Ekwall, Eldon, E., "Basic Sight Words" from *Locating and Correcting Reading Difficulties,* 4th edition (Columbus, OH: Charles E. Merrill Publishing Co., 1985), copyright © 1985 by Eldon E. Ekwall. Used with permission.

**1**

| | | | | | |
|---|---|---|---|---|---|
| know | down | water | my | good | will |
| one | here | be | the | in | oh |
| to | little | for | what | not | you |
| and | put | his | but | this | your |
| do | two | make | go | who | |
| her | away | said | I | come | |
| like | eat | we | no | has | |

*Primer:*

| | | | | | |
|---|---|---|---|---|---|
| about | all | an | as | blue | by |
| call | could | find | from | give | green |
| had | help | is | let | may | me |
| mother | old | other | ran | ride | sat |
| see | so | something | take | them | there |
| time | up | very | was | went | when |
| after | am | around | back | by | saw |
| came | day | fly | funny | green | they |
| he | how | jump | man | may | would |
| now | on | over | red | ride | yes |
| she | some | stop | that | them | |
| tree | us | want | way | went | |

*First Reader:*

| | | | | | |
|---|---|---|---|---|---|
| again | were | than | pull | name | side |
| boy | ask | why | their | read | took |
| fun | buy | ate | work | think | black |
| long | got | cold | been | door | fast |
| or | Mrs. | happy | cry | began | light |
| soon | please | morning | into | laugh | night |
| well | tell | pretty | must | never | sleep |
| any | white | thank | rabbit | shall | under |
| brown | at | with | these | thought | father |
| girl | children | ball | yellow | better | walk |
| Mr. | high | color | before | far | five |
| out | more | if | dog | light | four |
| stand | party | much | just | new | |

*2-1 Level:*

| | | | | | |
|---|---|---|---|---|---|
| always | end | head | once | sit | while |
| does | hand | near | should | warm | full |
| going | many | say | until | clean | last |
| live | right | together | bring | found | still |
| pick | thing | both | fall | keep | wish |
| sure | best | every | hot | our | gave |
| another | enough | hold | only | six | left |
| each | hard | next | show | which | year |
| grow | men | school | wait | cut | |
| made | round | told | carry | friend | |
| lace | those | box | first | kind | |
| ten | book | eye | hurt | own | |
| because | even | home | open | start | |

*2-2 Level:*

| | | | | | |
|---|---|---|---|---|---|
| dear | done | drink | off | most | people |
| seem | seven | sing | small | such | write |
| today | try | turn | use | wash | present |

*Third Reader Level:*

| | | | |
|---|---|---|---|
| also | eight | kind | upon |
| don't | goes | leave | grand |
| draw | its | myself | |

## A Supplement to the Dolch Word Lists[2]

| | | | | |
|---|---|---|---|---|
| 1. more | 15. world | 29. used | 43. united | 57. yet |
| 2. than | 16. still | 30. states | 44. left | 58. government |
| 3. other | 17. between | 31. himself | 45. number | 59. system |
| 4. such | 18. life | 32. few | 46. course | 60. set |
| 5. even | 19. being | 33. during | 47. war | 61. told |
| 6. most | 20. same | 34. without | 48. until | 62. nothing |
| 7. also | 21. another | 35. place | 49. something | 63. end |
| 8. through | 22. white | 36. American | 50. fact | 64. called |
| 9. years | 23. last | 37. however | 51. though | 65. didn't |
| 10. should | 24. might | 38. Mrs. | 52. less | 66. eyes |
| 11. each | 25. great | 39. thought | 53. public | 67. asked |
| 12. people | 26. year | 40. part | 54. almost | 68. later |
| 13. Mr. | 27. since | 41. general | 55. enough | 69. knew |
| 14. state | 28. against | 42. high | 56. took | |

A study of the words in any list will reveal two word classes: form words and function words. Form words are an open class of words consisting of nouns, verbs, adjectives, and adverbs. As new words enter the English language, this class expands. Function words, however, are a closed class of about 135 words. Articles, conjunctions, prepositions, and interjections comprise this category and differ from form words in that:

1. They usually have syntactical rather than lexical meaning and therefore are difficult to visualize or explain.
2. They occur over and over in written language. In the sentence "A boy went to the store," three of the six words—a, to, the—are function words.

For both reasons and because the sound–symbol relationship for function words is often irregular (*to, the, of, they*), it makes sense to teach function words as sight words.

A third source of sight words is words that students indicate a desire to know, often taken from language experience stories, Big Books, and poems. Students tend to learn the words they find meaningful more easily than words you select. High imagery words like *dinosaur* and *robot* (as opposed to *time* and *thing*) also tend to be learned and retained more readily.

---

[2]Johns, Jerry L. "A Supplement to the Dolch Word Lists." *Reading Improvement,* Winter 1971–1972, p. 91. Used with permission.

Whole language approaches focus on meeting words in context. Repeated readings and writing help to develop a growing sight vocabulary. However, most students need a great many repetitions before they automatically identify a word. Students progress through three stages to achieve sight word mastery: awareness that a word has been seen before, accuracy in pronouncing the word when it is met, and finally automaticity, in other words, saying the word without hesitation. To reinforce awareness of words met first in context, isolated word drill is often appropriate. This means that you must find varied and motivating ways to provide old-fashioned drill. In reading as in carpentry, drills are tools. In reading, they are tools for building fluency. A connected and fluent reading experience is our ultimate goal.

Although isolated skill practice may be valuable as an interim step, the reader should quickly be encouraged to recognize these isolated words in a single fixation when they are part of two or three word phrases. Phrase reading is an essential technique the fluent reader uses in connected reading, and it helps to discourage word-by-word reading. Words appearing in isolation *and* in context should be utilized both for instruction and for evaluating instruction. The Dolch list of sight phrases provides a model for the kind of phrase that may be useful for both purposes. Using similar phrases from the specific books that students are reading is still more effective.

### Dolch Sight Phrases[3]

| | | |
|---|---|---|
| can live | on the chair | is coming |
| down the hill | with mother | will go |
| will walk | down there | for the girl |
| in the barn | my father | if I must |
| they are | so much | as he did |
| if you can | his brother | when I wish |
| what I say | you will do | the small boy |
| all day | so long | it was |
| some bread | must be | down the street |
| you were | will buy | the red apple |
| to the farm | some cake | the little pig |
| her father | as I said | the little chicken |
| on the floor | too soon | with us |
| from the tree | what I want | would want |
| was made | I was | all night |
| at home | at once | her mother |
| the black horse | for them | is going |
| you will like | will think | it is |
| went away | the black bird | will read |
| in the window | a new hat | to the school |
| in the box | about it | they were |
| for him | he is | he was |
| I may go | to go | in the garden |

---

[3]Dolch, Edward, *Dolch Sight Phrases* (Champaign, IL: Garrard Publishing Co., 1949). Used with permission.

| | | |
|---|---|---|
| from home | we were | from the farm |
| the old men | the little dog | my brother |
| for the baby | at school | your sister |
| the new coat | by the tree | too little |
| a big horse | up here | I will come |
| then he came | would like | could make |
| by the house | went down | I will go |
| the old man | the yellow cat | to the barn |
| the small boat | up there | can fly |
| I am | the funny man | a big house |
| a pretty picture | I may get | about him |
| as I do | if you wish | then he said |
| he would try | can play | could eat |
| we are | has made | to the nest |
| a pretty home | when you know | did not fall |
| must go | in the grass | in the water |
| his sister | a new book | will look |
| if I may | the red cow | the yellow ball |
| you are | the little children | was found |
| did not go | to stop | your mother |
| has come back | when you come | can run |
| as he said | the new doll | to the house |
| the funny rabbit | when I can | the white sheep |
| as three | has found | |
| has run away | the white duck | |

## IDENTIFYING THE SKILL NEED

When students read orally, you are able to readily assess their sight vocabulary to determine whether they might benefit by sight word instruction or practice.

Students who read fluently are demonstrating automatic recognition of the words they are meeting. Students who read in a word-by-word fashion or hesitate before attempting "difficult" words may be analyzing the words and have not yet committed them to memory.

Some students misread function words—*a* for *the*, *in* for *on*—indicating either that: (1) these words are not automatic, or (2) one or more of the following words is taking their attention and is not yet learned by sight.

Students may repeat phrases preceding a troublesome word to gain time to decode the word.

Finally, some students may substitute words that do not necessarily disrupt meaning but which may show overreliance on context when certain words are unknown. Much of the time, however, when students substitute words that do not disrupt meaning, it may in fact be a sign of fluency. Students' eyes have moved ahead of their voices and they substitute a meaningful word because the material already read by their eyes has been comprehended and they have moved on.

*A CAUTION*    A number of assessment instruments claim to measure sight word knowledge by asking students to choose the visual representation of a word you pronounce. Usually three or four choices are shown, with the distractors varying in difficulty.

*EXAMPLE*    You read, "Circle the word *guess*."

guest
guess
guessed
gas

Although this kind of assessment is easy to administer because it can be done with the group as a whole, it is not asking the student to demonstrate the production skills needed in reading sight words. In a real reading situation, the students must indicate that they know the pronunciation of a word by naming it rather than merely recognizing it. Success with this kind of typical exercise does not guarantee sight word knowledge of the words used.

## TEACHING THE SKILL: TECHNIQUES AND ACTIVITIES

Because it is important to build students' vocabulary, there are a few guidelines that are useful to follow.

1.   Words that you expect students to learn should be a part of their speaking/listening vocabularies.
2.   Be sure that students are not presented with too many sight words in one lesson and that they have enough exposure to the words to commit them to memory.
3.   Help students to focus on the word. Sometimes students look up at you to have words pronounced instead of looking at the words as they are read, or they may focus on the beginning letter or on another recognizable part of the word rather than looking at the whole word.
4.   If students confuse words that are similar in appearance, it may be useful to show both words together so that you can highlight the differences.

### FOCUS ON WORD MEANINGS

Students' ability to relate to a word's meaning has been shown to influence the ease with which they learn the word. Be sure your students know the meanings of the words they are learning to read and can use the words correctly.

In choosing sight words to introduce, words occurring in materials read to students offer an obvious source. You might try to cluster words around similar themes or meanings from these stories. Animal words, color words, and sports words are examples. From the book *Big Red Barn* (Brown, 1989), you might use the phrases: *big red barn, great green field, pink pig, golden flying horse, big white hen, big brown cow, old black cat, old red dog, little black bats.*

Chapter 6 offers suggestions for building meaning vocabulary. Many of these techniques for generating vocabulary provide opportunities that foster sight vocabulary building as well.

### SHARED READING EXPERIENCES

Shared reading experiences that attempt to mimic home lap reading, where the same book is read and reread, translate to the classroom when you read from a Big

Book placed on an easel for all the students to see. Big Books with their rhymes, predictable plot, and/or repetitive phrases that encourage multiple readings with students joining in, offer sight word building opportunities. With each rereading you may wish to highlight certain words or phrases. The words from the text may then be further used with many of the suggestions below.

### WORDS ON DISPLAY

Words students are learning may be written in large letters on cards and placed alphabetically high up on the walls. Charts with words that center around a theme or book may also be used (as in the *Big Red Barn* example). If classroom activities include reference to and use of these words, they will foster sight recognition.

### FIND THE LUCKY NUMBER

Experiment with students to determine the number of sight words that can be learned in one sitting and remembered the next day. Do not attempt to teach more than this number in a single lesson. It's conceivable that this number will be "one" at first; however, slow but steady progress is preferable to no progress. As students acquire a larger repertoire of sight words, their learning capacity may increase. Continuing evaluation is important.

### BANKING WORDS

You may wish to make a word box or word bank for each student. As words are presented to students, they write each word on a 3" × 5" card. They may illustrate the word if possible, and then they should write the word on the back of the card with a sentence using the word. The illustrated side of the card is for learning the word; the back of the card is for testing the student. Students may work in pairs to quiz each other. Divide the box into two sections, and as words are learned they should be entered into the "learned" section (to be distinguished from the "working on" section). Students enjoy seeing the learned section grow steadily. These words can be used for all of the practice ideas listed later in the chapter.

*VARIATION* Keep the words that the students are working on in their word boxes. As they learn the words, have the students write them on circle coin cards (25¢, 10¢, 5¢, 1¢) that they can deposit into piggy banks made of boxes without a top. Paste the picture of a pig to the side of the box. A slit must be made in the pig's body to bank the "coins." The students can review their words by reading them and counting their money. Harder words should go on coins of greater value.

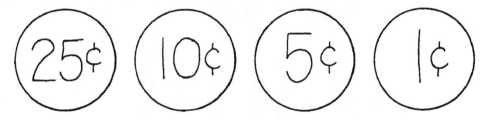

### TRACE AND READ

1. Some students need to trace or write the word as well as say, see, and hear it. Have students trace over the word at the board using colored chalk. A color felt-tip pen may be used if tracing the word on a piece of paper. Then have the students write the word themselves, always saying the word at the finish.

2. Tracing the word in a low box filled with dry, flavored gelatin helps students get the feel of the letters in the word. This kind of kinesthetic approach often is helpful to the slower learner who needs lots of sensory input. Licking fingers afterward is a reward, let's hope second only to the thrill of learning! Have the students write words with finger paints if you don't mind the mess.

3. Writing missing letters of the word and tracing over the others, eventually leading to writing the whole word, is good practice for some students. They read the word aloud each time.

*EXAMPLE*    He is *the* boy.

    _ he

    __ e

    ___

If the words are done on laminated cards, they may be used again.

### CUT AND SORT

Have students write each word on two cards. Cut apart the letters of the word on the first card, mix them up, and have the student reassemble the word. Students can match their efforts to the second card. This may also be done with sentences. The words from the sentence may be cut apart and students then reassemble the jumbled sentence. Finally, students should read the completed word or sentence.

### SPELLING TO JOG MEMORY

For some students, spelling out the letters of the word and then immediately pronouncing it is helpful as a beginning crutch. The spelling triggers the memory of the word. Eventually, the spelling is dropped.

## VISUALIZE THE WORD

Have the students look carefully at the word and then to try and see it with their eyes closed, perhaps even writing the word in the air and pronouncing and/or spelling it with eyes still closed. The students may then open their eyes, check the word again and proceed to write the word on paper with eyes open, again simultaneously pronouncing the word.

## CALL ATTENTION TO ALL PARTS OF THE WORD

Many students fixate on the beginnings of words. When they are learning color words individually, for example, they easily learn *blue,* and then *black* or even *brown.* Once all three words have been taught, however, seeing *blue* can easily evoke a response of "black" or "brown." Try to encourage students to focus on features in the middle and endings of words as well as in their beginnings. Ask "How are these words alike and how are they different?"

## FEATURE THE FEATURES

In teaching a sight word, have students participate in a discussion of its meaning and distinguishing visual features. Ask the students to think about and tell you how they can best remember the word. In searching for these distinguishing features, their memory will be enhanced.

*EXAMPLE*    One student explained that she could distinguish between *want* and *went* because she *wants* an ant farm and *ant* is in *want* but not in *went.*

## DISTINGUISH VISUALLY SIMILAR WORDS

1. Use a homemade tachistoscope to practice these words in isolation or in phrases *(bother, brother; through, through, thought)*. The tachistoscope may be an animal head with the visually similar words appearing in the eyes or the phrase in the mouth.
2. Help students utilize context for determining a word by providing sentences missing the sight word. Give visually similar words to choose from.

*EXAMPLE*    The boy went _____ the door.
   though      through

3. Have students find a sight word in a word search. Use visually similar words as distractors. Have the student trace the word with a color felt-tip pen rather than circle it. For students who have visual problems or a learning disability, this type of activity may be frustrating and therefore not appropriate.

*EXAMPLE*    B T H O U G H D F P A


   T H G H T H R O U G H


   O U G H T T H O U G H

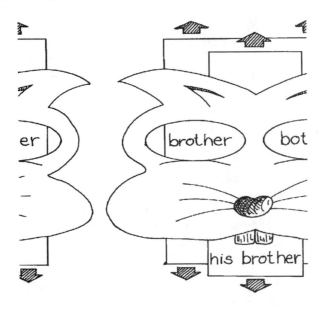

## MULTIPLYING SIGHT WORDS

When you are teaching a verb—the word *jump*, for example—it is a good idea to show students the words *jumps, jumped,* and *jumping* so that the students understand from the start that inflecting the root will enable them to read a great many more words. You might want to encourage students to cover an *ing, s,* or *ed* at the end of an inflected word with their fingers to facilitate identifying the root.

## FUNCTION WORDS PRACTICE

1. Have the students use one or two long articles from the front page of the newspaper and circle every *of* or *the*, pronouncing the word each time they circle it. This should be done quickly. A timer may be used. The students may count the number of times *of* appears. They can then try it with *was, in, on,* or another frequently appearing word and can compare scores.
2. Create a number of simple phrases using the function words (*at the top, in the hole, to a boy, for her mom*). Be sure the noun used is an easy, familiar one. Have students flip through the phrases with a timer, trying to improve their speed. Since function words appear in 50 percent of most printed text, it is important that they can be read automatically.

## PROVIDE NUMEROUS AND VARIED REPETITIONS

Use the books students are reading as your source of sight words.

1. Many games that practice sight words require pairs of cards. Having students make the second or matching set of cards for games like "Go Fish," "Concentration," or "Old Maid" provides additional motivating reinforcement.
2. Have a ring (notebook type) that can open and attach to a student's belt loop. Put sight word cards on the ring each day. At several points during the day, have students read their words to you or to each other. Have the students bring the ring home each night to practice reading the words.

3. Give each student a word to read for the day. As students leave the classroom for recess, lunch, gym, or changing classes, they quickly read their words to you.

4. For appropriate words, have students individually read a word card and act out the word for the others to guess.

5. *Board games.* A number of different kinds of board games allow the student to read aloud the sight word, phrase, or sentence in order to move or advance toward winning the game.
   Examples include:
   a. Any kind of game in which words or phrases are written on the board or appear in packs of cards. The students move the appropriate number of spaces. If they can read the word on the space or the card they've picked, they stay there and continue on at their next turn. If they can't read the word, they go back to the previous space.
   b. Football fields, baseball fields, checkerboards, spaces leading to an airplane hangar, a ladder top, or just a plain board with an interesting shape. The board shape may be suggested by the book from which the words are taken. The words, phrases, or sentences from *My Grandma's Chair* (Maggie Smith, 1992) may be placed on a board that has a large armchair drawn on it.

*A HELPFUL HINT*   If word packs are used, each student may pick on his/her own pack so that the word practice may be individualized.

6. *Chance reading*
   a. Students working alone or in pairs may reach into a bag and pick a card. If they can read the word, phrase, or sentence, they keep it. You might label each bag with the name of a book they've read and put the words or sentences from the book inside. For class written language experience stories, sentences might have the author of each sentence following it, for example: Today we went apple picking. (Tom)
   b. You hold up word cards. If students can read them, they keep them. A variation has cards with directions—for example, "Jump up and down." If students can do what the cards say, they keep the cards.
   c. Students fish with a pole to which string and a magnet are attached. Cards shaped like fish each have a paperclip on them. The magnet pulls up a card which can be kepf if read correctly. Cards may have words or sentences from stories on them. Students may try to guess which story the sentences are from.
   In all instances, the winner is the student with the most cards.

7. *Self-checking devices*
   a. A board can have flaps stapled at the top with colors, numbers, or picturable nouns written on each flap. As the students read each word, they check the accuracy by picking up the flap to see the circle of color, number, or picture under the flap.

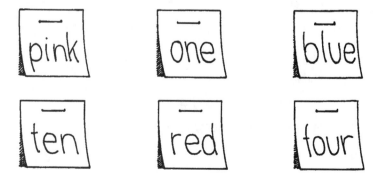

b. Students may place lists of words or phrases on strips for individual tachistoscopes. After practicing the words, the students turn on a teacher-made tape recording of the list and listen to see if they were correct.

## READ, READ, READ

1. Easy reading materials that frequently repeat words help students see sight words in context and gain automaticity. Don't be afraid to let students read easy material. It builds sight word knowledge as well as success.
2. Reading partners may read a book together chorally, then take turns reading a book a page at a time, and finally switch pages for a third reading. The repeated readings help to cement the vocabulary, and the partners are able to cue each other when necessary.
3. Listening to a book on tape while following along in the book and then reading along with the tape provides much the same benefit as reading with a live partner and can be repeated indefinitely.
4. Rereading a book several times in anticipation of taping it offers opportunity for building automaticity.
5. Have students reread or read their choice of book to the class. This means preparing by practicing and perhaps taping.

## WRITE, WRITE, WRITE

1. Every time students write words, they are strengthening their sight recognition of these words. It makes sense to give children opportunities to write daily, such as journal writing, describing a drawing, letter or note writing, or making word bank cards. If students keep writing dictionaries of the words they use that they have needed help with and/or words are displayed on the walls that students are encouraged to use as a resource for their writing, sight recognition of these words is further reinforced.
2. Class or group structured language experience activities in which the first part of the sentence is kept constant build recognition of high-frequency words.

*EXAMPLE*     I like to play _____

I like to play _____

I like to play _____

or

The daily story:

Today is *(day, date)*.

It is a *(weather adjective)* day.

We are *(activity for day)*.

Books like *Martha Matilda O'Toole* (Jim Copp, 1969) do the same thing.

"Martha Matilda's forgotten her book."
"Martha Matilda's forgotten her pen."
"Martha Matilda's forgotten her shoes."
"Martha Matilda's forgotten her dress."

NAME: **Don't Get Behind the Eight Ball**

SKILL: Reading sight words

MATERIALS: Game board, two packs of cards (12 in each pack)

PROCEDURE:
1.  Have one pack of sight words that students have learned easily (Easy pack). Each word card is written in blue. The other pack should have the sight words that have been difficult to learn (Demon pack). Each of these should be written in red.
2.  The students each spin the die and move the number of spaces indicated by the die. If the space they move to has one star, they pick from the easy pack. Reading the word correctly earns them one point. If the space has two stars, students pick from the demon pack and receive two points for reading the word correctly. Play continues to the space marked END.
3.  The student with the most points at the end wins.

VARIATION: You may use this board to develop a skill for which you can devise easy and hard items (words to practice vowels, synonyms and antonyms, etc.). You may also ignore the easy and demon designations and use different skills for the pack (e.g., demon sight words and context sentences or words to practice vowels, etc.).

# DON'T GET BEHIND
# THE EIGHT BALL

*NAME:* **Go Fly a Kite**

*SKILL:* Reading sight phrases

*MATERIALS:* Game board, ten different colored pens or crayons

*PROCEDURES:*
1. Use ten phrases (those below are from the Dolch list of sight phrases), one on each kite.
2. On each tail, print a word or phrase that completes the phrase on one of the kites.
3. Have the students use ten different colored crayons and draw lines from each kite to its appropriate tail.
4. If you wish to put this game on a worksheet, the students may use string and glue in place of crayons.

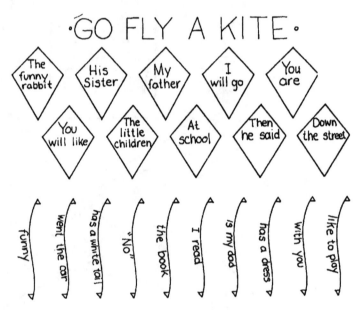

*VARIATIONS:* This game may be used with any skill for which you can devise pairs of words or sentences.

vowel symbol (a)—vowel word (cat)
prefixes and/or suffixes—roots
synonyms—antonyms
words—definitions, synonymous phrases
cause—effect

Context or multiple meaning: The kites and tails may have pairs of sentences that can be completed by filling in the same word for each. The first kite might have the sentence: He hit the _____ . The sentence on the appropriate tail might read: She danced at the _____ . The word *ball* would fit both sentences.

1. She can _____ fast.
   The stocking has a _____ in it. *(run)*

2. Will you _____ that out to me?
   The pencil has a sharp _____ . *(point)*

3. He lit the _____ .
   Does this shirt _____ the pants? *(match)* etc.

Other possibilities in sentences: *star, crack, jar, trip, fair, play.*

GO FLY A KITE.

17

# 2

# Phonic Analysis

## DESCRIBING THE SKILL

How much phonics instruction belongs in the teaching of reading? The answer to this question varies from teacher to teacher. The expert reader is a sight reader and relies very little, if at all, on phonics. However, for most beginners, a certain amount of phonics is necessary to develop independent reading.

Most phonics teaching begins with consonant sounds. Consonants provide the "backbone" of words. "C_n y_ r_d th_s?" is probably decodable for most readers, whereas "_a_ _ou _ea_ _ _i_?" is not. To work successfully with consonant letters and sounds, students must first be able to identify the sound of the consonant letter when it is found in the initial, medial, or final position in a word. Consonant digraphs *(ch, gh, ph, sh, th, wh, ng)* are taught and reinforced in an identical manner to individual consonants. Like individual consonants, they produce a single sound, and blending of sounds, which is a more difficult task, is not necessary. With consonant clusters, students learn to blend together the two or three individual sounds.

Vowels are more unpredictable than consonants. Individual vowel letters may represent several different sounds. The letter *o*, for example, sounds different in the words *hot, through, home, out,* and *orange.* Moreover, a vowel sound may be spelled in a number of ways. Long *e* can be spelled in any one of seven ways as seen in the words: *see, sea, Pete, receive, he, believe, key.* There are, however, syllable patterns that indicate that a particular vowel sound is likely (CVC, CVCe, etc.). Yet these patterns, though helpful, are rarely without exceptions. It is essential to teach students to be flexible decoders. When one vowel sound produces a nonsense word, a student should be ready to try another vowel sound.

You may prefer to teach vowels as parts of word patterns called phonograms, word families, or the rhyming part. These all refer to the part of a one-syllable word that begins with the vowel (*bat, plate, star, tall, pail, raw,* etc.). The phonogram in an unknown word *(brat)* is compared to a known word *(cat)* with the same phonogram. By applying consonant substitution, the unfamiliar word can now be decoded. The issue of whether the vowel is long, short, or irregular is moot.

Decide on your approach to phonics. Will you use whole words to demonstrate letter sounds or phonograms (analytic phonics), sounds in isolation that you will then help students to blend (synthetic phonics /b/ /a/ /t/ = /bat/ or /b/ /at/ ), or a combination? Some of you may prefer a formal phonics program that can coordinate with spelling. Others may use language experience class stories, Big Books, or children's oral reading or writing as your impetus for teaching phonics.

## IDENTIFYING THE SKILL NEED

Students' ability to use decoding skills effectively to aid word identification may be observed in their connected oral reading performance, in their writing, or tested directly through the use of formal or informal phonics instruments. An occasional error does not indicate lack of a phonics skill. Rather, patterns of error may reveal the need for phonics instruction. One consonant, for example, may be omitted regularly from consonant clusters. Particular vowel combinations (*taut, haul, pound, shout*) may be continually mispronounced.

The need for phonics instruction may also be shown when students demonstrate difficulty with irregular words where the vowel sound differs from the rule or pattern they expect—*come*, for example, may be pronounced like *home*. Some students may show you a need for attention to letters and letter sounds when they read words that are appropriate to the meaning of the text but do not conform to the actual written word. "Mark drove the automobile into the parking lot" becomes "Mark drove the cab. . . ."

Students' writing offers opportunities to see where phonics instruction might be useful. Many of you may be encouraging your K–2 students to write using invented spelling (i.e., to write the sounds they hear: I km ovr yer hos). A careful analysis of their efforts will help you to see what sound–symbol correspondences they've mastered and where instruction is needed.

*A CAUTION*   When you are working with students, you might ask them to find a word in their books that rhymes with or has the same vowel sound as a word that you have pronounced. Do not assume that because students are able to do this that they necessarily know the sound in question. This is different from real reading, which asks students to pronounce the word independently. The first task is important as an initial step but, when you are checking phonics knowledge, be sure that you have asked students to produce sounds or words themselves before making the judgment that a particular sound–symbol relationship is known.

## TEACHING THE SKILL: TECHNIQUES AND ACTIVITIES

When you are teaching phonics, there are a few guidelines that may be helpful:

1. Try not to teach too many sounds at one time. In your attempt to get through all of the reading material you feel you need to in a school day, you may teach too much too fast. Moreover, a student's ability to display short-term memory skills may trick you into believing that a skill has been learned permanently. As you forge ahead, the student falls further and further behind.
2. Remember to teach phonemic awareness first. Some students may have trouble separating one sound from another within a word.
3. Teach students to be flexible decoders. Students who try, for example, to pronounce the word *fĭnd* as *find* need to be encouraged to try different vowel sounds until the word makes sense, especially if the alternative vowel sound doesn't conform to rules they've learned.

4.  When you are teaching phonics, remember to remind students that they must continue to use context clues to confirm their attempts at phonic analysis. For example, in the sentence "He was wearing a *bow* tie," *bow* may be read incorrectly to rhyme with *cow*.

The techniques described below begin with suggestions for help with individual sounds both in isolation and within words, continue with hints for blending sounds within words, and finally move to words in larger thought units—phrases, sentences, and paragraphs.

## KNOW WHERE YOU'RE GOING, PROCEED STEP BY STEP, AND DON'T RUSH

1.  Decide on the sequence of sounds you will teach.
2.  Progress systematically, making certain students have success with a sound before teaching a new one.
3.  Provide continued practice with old sounds when new sounds are taught.
4.  If you have isolated words, put them back into context as quickly as possible, and always discuss a word's meaning to ensure that students recognize the word they have sounded.
5.  Provide connected reading to practice sounds in context.

## HELP STUDENTS LEARN SOUND–SYMBOL RELATIONSHIPS

1.  Use pictures that highlight a letter's configuration. When possible, give students pictures that begin with a letter and remind them of its written form and sound.

You can't always find a picture that mimics the letter's shape, but pictures can serve as key words. Display the pictures in the classroom to serve as reminders of sound and symbol. Emphasize that the letter name and letter sound usually differ. (The letter *b* is pronounced "bee," but the sound of the letter *b* is /b/ ).

Equally effective is the use of character names from the books you are reading to and with students in the classroom to cue letters and sounds. Beady Bear (*Beady Bear*, Freeman, 1954), for example, may serve as a reminder for the letter *B*. Have students make letter pages for a dictionary. At the top of each letter page, have them draw a picture of the appropriate literature character with the name written beside it, underlining or coloring the initial letters (in this case, the *B*).

2.  Practice having students identify sounds within words.

**a.** Have students write the letter they hear at the beginning (middle end) of each of these words: *bad, rug, pot, sill, tub, den.*

**b.** Make class or group collages for letters. Have students paste pictures that begin (end) with the sound on a large sheet of paper. The letter may be painted on afterward and the collage displayed in the room. Students may also draw pictures from a book they're reading or being read. For example, *How Does the Wind Walk?* (Carlstrom, 1993) offers a number of words that begin with *w.*

**c.** Make posters of letters with pockets into which the students can place cut-out pictures that begin or end with the letter sound. Medial vowels can also be used, as can phonograms. At various points in the day or week, you can sort through the pictures with the students to reinforce the sound and correct errors.

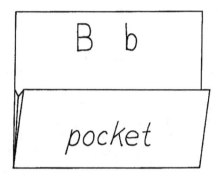

**d.** *Picture cards.* (1) Prepare picture cards with the beginning, ending, vowel letter, or phonogram written on the back (e.g., A picture of a cat may have a *c,* an *a,* a *t,* or an *at* written on the back). Have two students work together to test each other. (2) Give students laminated pictures with space beneath the picture to write the initial, vowel, final letter, or phonogram. Have the students say aloud what the picture shows before writing the appropriate grapheme(s). You may have the grapheme(s) written on the back for self-checking.

**e.** *Bat a Round.* Place a picture of a baseball bat on one side of an oaktag folder with letters written in spaces around the perimeter of the bat. The other side of the folder should have two pipe cleaners attached to it with the headings *Cards* and *Used Cards,* respectively. Picture cards representing phonograms, or initial, final, or vowel sounds are placed on the *Cards* pipe cleaner. Students take turns moving one space at a time and picking a picure card. If the card matches the letter in the space (for phonogram, or initial, final or vowel sound—any one or any combination may be used), the students keep the card. Otherwise, it goes on the *Used Cards* pile. When the cards are used up, the students play with the *Used Cards* pile. The student with the most cards at the end wins. One student may play alone to see if he or she can better a previous score. The shape used for the folder may be taken from a book the students are reading. For example, instead of using a bat, a snake may be drawn and appropriate pictures from *Crictor* (Ungerer, 1958) that illustrate particular sounds may be placed on the pipe cleaners.

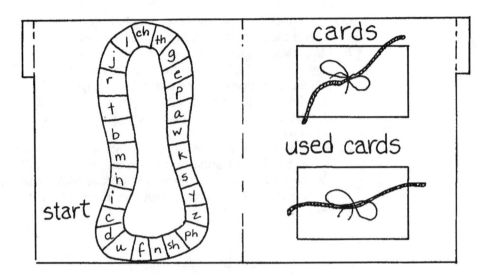

f. *Climbing Up.* A ladder is drawn diagonally on one side of the oaktag folder with pipe cleaners attached to each rung. The other side of the folder has two attached pipe cleaners headed *Letters* and *Pictures.* Cards for each are placed on the appropriate pipe cleaners. Students place a letter card at the top of the ladder. They then look for pictures that begin with the sound the letter represents and place one on each rung. (Ending sounds, vowel sounds, and phonograms may also be used.) Pictures may have the relevant letter written on the back for self-checking. Again, the pictures may come from a book the class is reading or being read.

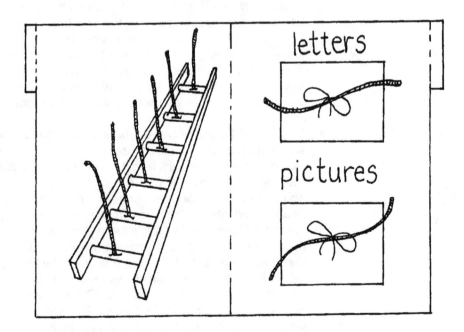

g. *Word chains.* Write and/or read a word that begins with a particular letter. Have the students volunteer another word that begins or ends the same way.

The game may be played this way. Say a word (e.g., *bat*). A student must give a word that begins with the ending sound of *bat* (e.g., *top*). Continue in this fashion.

## TEACH DIGRAPHS AND CLUSTERS IN THE INITIAL POSITION FIRST

1. Show students that when consonants combine with *h* (*ch, ph, sh, th,*) a brand new sound results, different from either letter alone. Use pictures or sound images to reinforce the sound. *Ch, ch, ch, ch*—*choo choo train; sh, sh*—*quiet; th*—tongue between your teeth; *wh*—whistle (purse your lips).
2. Have students read the words *sip* and *lip*. Then combine the *s* and *l* to make *slip*. Do this with each of the clusters so that the students see how the cluster is formed.
3. Form cluster wheels in two steps. To teach *l* or *r* clusters, have a center word such as *lack* or *rack*. Have an outer wheel with single consonants that turns to form words with the center word. Then proceed to a center wheel with the phonogram *ack* and the clusters on the outer wheel.

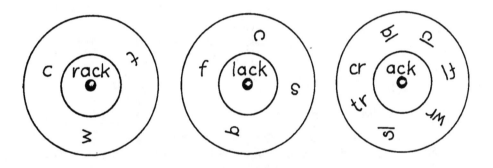

4. You might wish to play "one sound or two" with students. As you flash a card with a consonant digraph *(ch)* or a consonant cluster *(cl)*, students may state whether these letters generally refer to one or two sounds. You might ask for a word that demonstrates their response.

## FOR SOME STUDENTS, LEARNING THE VOWEL GENERALIZATIONS PROVES USEFUL

It is helpful to remember that these generalizations apply to syllables. Since most beginning reading words have one syllable, the generalizations are applicable right from the beginning. Always help the students to use the generalizations flexibly, recognizing that exceptions are rarely the exception. Useful rules to teach include:

1. When there is one vowel at the end of a word or syllable, it is usually long (*gō, nā/tion*).
2. When there is one vowel in a word or syllable that is not the final letter and it is not followed by an *r*, it is usually short (*add, best, trip, hot, trust, gym*).
3. A vowel followed by an *r* has neither the long nor short sound (*her, car*).
4. When there are two vowels in a syllable, the first one is often long and the second one is silent (*rain, like*).

5.   Y has the long *i* sound when it is the only vowel in a one-syllable word and is the final letter of the word *(sky)*.

In words of two or more syllables, the final *y* preceded by a consonant has the sound of long *e* (*baby, happily*). When *y* is preceded by a vowel, it is usually part of a vowel digraph or diphthong (*play, key, toy*).

The following table shows syllable patterns useful in determining vowel sounds.

*Syllable Patterns**

| Short | Long | Other Sound |
|---|---|---|
| vc | cv | vr |
| cvc | cvce (usually long) sometimes short) | *aw, au, al* |
|  |  | *oi, oy, ou* *ow* (as in *owl*) |
|  | cvvc (usually for *ai, ay, ee, ea, oa;* sometimes for *oe, ow* (Note: *ea* often has short sound—*ow* can have sound heard in *owl*) | *oo* (both long and short variant— *book, moon*) |

## CLIMBING LADDERS

Have students read up and down vowel ladders to show how the vowel changes the word. The words on the ladder should conform to syllabic patterns. Explain that some of the words will be nonsense words.

| | | |
|---|---|---|
| bag | ha | make |
| beg | he | meke |
| big | hi | mike |
| bog | ho | moke |
| bug | hu | muke |

## REINFORCE VOWEL SOUNDS

1.   Using one sound at a time, have students read a number of words using that sound.

*EXAMPLE*   short vowel /ă/—*bat, bag, bad, man, map, cap, dam*

Many of the books the students are reading have words that reinforce a particular vowel sound. Karen Schmidt's *The Gingerbread Man* (1985) has numbers of short *a* words. Galdone's *The Little Red Hen* (1973) may be used for short *e*, and Keats' *Whistle for Willie* (1964) is appropriate for short *i* words.

---

*v = any vowel, c = any consonant.

2. Contrast two sounds using minimal pairs.
   **a.** short vowels

*EXAMPLE*    *mat, met,* etc.

   **b.** Silent *e (vce)*

*EXAMPLE*    *cap/cape, pet/Pete,* etc.

   **c.** vowel digraphs

*EXAMPLE*    *ran/rain, men/mean, got/goat, red/reed, pan/pawn/ Hal/haul,* etc.

   **d.** *r*-controlled vowels

*EXAMPLE*    *cat/cart, chip/chirp,* etc.

## HERE'S HOW

1. Vowels are often taught through the use of rhyme by using phonograms.
   **a.** Most competent readers automatically identify unknown words by relating the word to a similar known word. Help students to see that when words sound the same at the end (rhyme), they often look the same *(cat, hat)*.
   **b.** Teach them to recognize the familiar ending *(at)* in an unfamiliar word *(chat)* by recalling a word with that ending *(cat)*.
   **c.** Use consonant substitution to read the new word. You may wish to practice consonant substitution rhyming by using word families to build words. Teach the students two or three word phonograms *(at, en, ill, ot,* etc.) and have them try to make real or nonsense words by blending a consonant, consonant digraph, or consonant cluster to the beginning (i.e., *dat, den, dill dot*). Using homemade anagrams can be an effective way of practicing this. Cut one-inch squares of oaktag and write a separate letter on each square. Have many squares for each letter, especially the vowels.

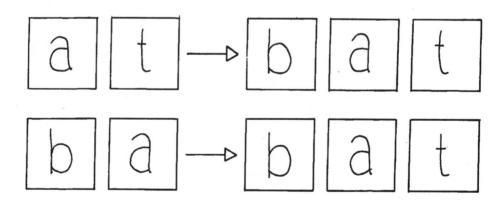

   **d.** Try teaching students to separate phonograms from initial sound and then blend them by clapping them together. The students say the initial sound looking at their left hand and then the phonogram looking at their right hand. They then say the word clapping the sounds and their hands together.

    **e.** Post known key words on the board *(cat, name, bed, hill, pot)* to practice the technique (identifying an unknown word by relating the phonogram to a known rhyming word and using consonant substitution).

**2.** Ignore vowels. Show students that it is not always necessary to recall vowel sounds. Often using context and the consonants is enough. Can you read this b___k? Have students work with partners writing sentences with missing vowels.

**3.** If vowels are particularly problematic, it may be useful to provide a method or sequence for word attack. Have the student: (1) identify the vowel sound first, (2) add the ending, and (3) blend in the initial grapheme.

*EXAMPLE*    cat = ă at cat
bake = ā ake bake
rest = ĕ est rest

    This is not appropriate for students who have problems with left–hand sequencing (see Chapter 5).

**4.** Show students how to use their knowledge of vowel sounds flexibly. When the expected pronunciation of an unknown word does not work, have students try another vowel sound. If in the sentence, *He ate the bread,* long *e* (brēd) does not work, have them try short *e* (brĕd). When neither long *e* nor short *e* decode *break,* have them try other vowel sounds until the word is discovered.

*EXAMPLE*    Please don't *break* that.

    *brēk, brĕk, brăk, brĭk*—Oh, I know—*brāk.*

## TAKE SOME TIPS FROM PUBLISHED READING SERIES

Many students who know letter sounds cannot blend them to form words without instruction. Following are some older approaches that are still useful.

**1.** Begin to practice blending with vowels and consonants that are continuants like *m, n, r, s.* Write the word *am.* Point to the *a* and have the child give the short sound and hold it. Then, without taking a breath, add the *m* sound. Next have the child say the word quickly. Demonstrate if necessary. Continue with *in, on.* Proceed to words beginning with a consonant such as *man, Sam.* Have the child hold the first letter and add successive letters without taking a breath. Then say the word quickly. (See the Lippincott *Basic Reading* Series, Book A, McCracken and Walcutt, 1975, for a complete description of this approach.)

**2.** Continue the one-breath procedure by having three children stand up, each holding a card to form a word such as *man.* Have the first child pronounce the *m* sound and bump up against the second who adds the *a* sound and bumps up against the third who adds the *n* sound. The word is then pronounced quickly. (See *Alpha One,* Reiss and Friedman, 1982, for a more complete description of this approach.)

**3.** If kids get stuck on slow decoding, use the DISTAR method of "say it fast." (*DISTAR Reading,* Englemann and Bruner, 1983.) Students slowly sound out the letters in a word (sss aaa mmm) and then blend the sounds by saying them fast (Sam).

### BASEBALL CATCH BLENDING

Using an oaktag folder, draw or paste a baseball glove on one side with an empty pipe cleaner attached to the palm. On the other side, attach to a pipe cleaner a number of laminated balls with a narrow oaktag slide that can be woven through two cuts in the center of each ball. On one side of the slide, write single consonants, and place consonant digraphs and clusters on the reverse side. Next to the two cuts on the ball, write a phonogram that will produce words when combined with the initial letters on the slide. The slide may be used on some balls to provide either the final consonant or the vowel by varying the placement of the cuts and the letters written on the ball. If students can read words on a ball that can be made by pulling the slide, they put the ball on the pipe cleaner on the glove and have "caught" that ball.

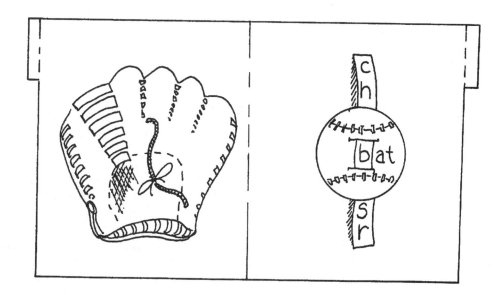

### WORDS IN PHRASES AND SENTENCES

Put words into phrases and sentences to practice letter sounds. Be sure students recognize that they must use context to confirm their analysis of a word. Have students respond to the sentences in various ways.

*EXAMPLE*   Make a silly or serious face after each sentence.

Bob bit the bug.
Chip can chop wood for a chair.
Green grapes grow in gravy.
Big Tim will hit with his fist.

Write "yes" or "no" after each sentence.

| | |
|---|---|
| Can you cut a cord? | Yes |
| Can ships shout? | No |
| Are blue and black colors? | Yes |
| Can you bake a game? | No |

## ANALYZE WORDS IN SENTENCES

Using sentences such as *Sam has a cap*, ask the child why the underlined word can't be hat, emphasizing that though the context and general size of the word fit, attention must be given to letters too.

## BACK TO BOOKS

Practice the elements being taught by choosing trade books that illustrate these particular sounds. Some examples were given earlier in this chapter. Two publishing companies that put out small storybooks written expressly to do this are listed below:

*Primary Phonics*, Educators Publishing Service, Inc., Cambridge, MA. (1995)
*Discovery Phonics*, Modern Curriculum Press, Cleveland, OH. (1992)

A variation would be to write your own short story (book) using the appropriate phonic elements. Leave the hero or heroine's name blank so students may fill in their own (_____ *had a sad cat*, etc.) Students like to read about themselves. Laminate the pages so that the book may be used by everyone. When students finish the book, they wipe off their names.

## PHONICS THROUGH WRITING

Students encouraged to use invented spelling present opportunities to explore sounds and the various letters that represent these sounds. Use words from the students' writing for charts or posters illustrating particular phonograms or vowel or consonant sounds.

Have the students keep writing dictionaries. As you work with specific words from their writing, have them add the words to the appropriate alphabet page.

# Activities to Go

*NAME:* **Be a Star**

*SKILL:* Consonant digraphs, consonant blends, blending

*MATERIALS:* Game board, die, board markers, paper, and pencil

*PROCEDURE:* The major purpose of this game is to build real and nonsense words. To do this, the students roll the die to see (1) how many spaces to move, and (2) which phonogram to use.

1. Fill in the star spaces and phonograms on the game board as shown.
2. A six on the die would have the student move six spaces to the beginning consonant cluster *fl*. The student would also use the phonogram *un* to build the nonsense word *flun*. The word is written and then pronounced.
3. At the end, the students read all of their words, indicating which are real words.
4. The game may result in different winners. One can be the student who finishes first. A second can be the student with the greatest number of real words.

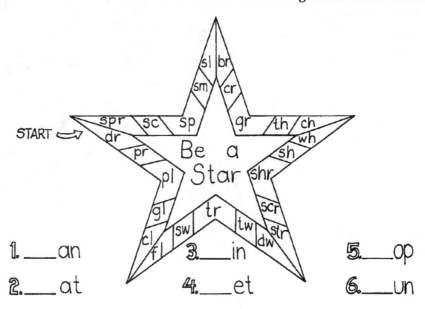

1. ___an
2. ___at
3. ___in
4. ___et
5. ___op
6. ___un

*VARIATIONS:* This game may be played with all elements that allow word or sentence building.

a. Use single consonants on the star spaces.
b. Use vowels and/or vowel digraphs on the star spaces. Instead of phonograms use six small words missing the vowel: *b_d, m_t, r_d, h_l, b_t, l_m*
c. Use root words like the following on the star spaces:
   lock, help, love, appear, fit,
   read, care, place, work, arm,
   color, tie, mind, joy, close,
   join, taste, prove, fear, play,
   pack, like, do, cover, comfort
   Use six prefixes and suffixes instead of phonograms:
   *dis-, un-, -ful, re-, -less, -able*

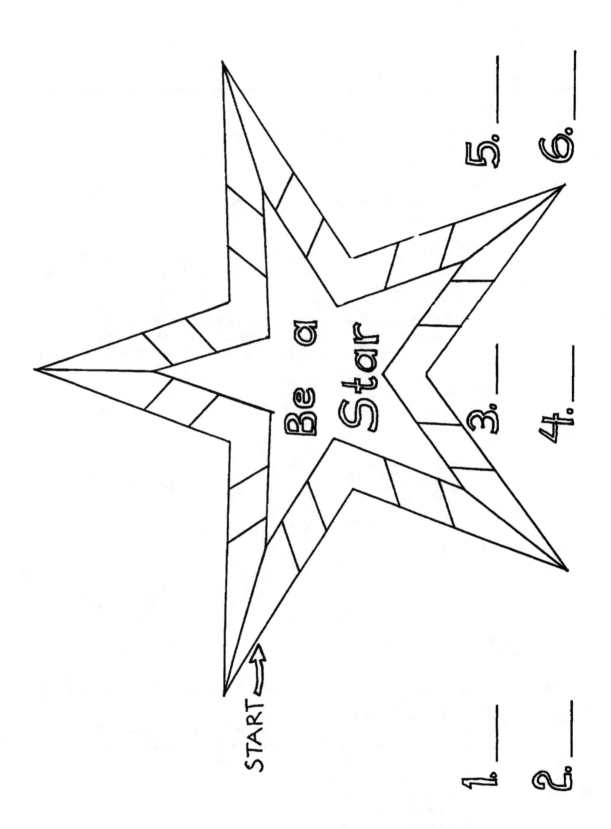

START

Be a
Star

1. ___
2. ___
3. ___
4. ___
5. ___
6. ___

| NAME: | **Fishy Words** |
|---|---|
| *SKILL:* | Consonants, vowels, blending |
| *MATERIALS:* | Game board, two spinners (a. 1-6; b. 1-3), markers, paper, and pencil |
| *PROCEDURE:* | Three letter words are written on the squares of the fish as shown below. The students use the spinner with numbers 1 to 6 to see how many spaces to move. The second spinner (1 to 3) is then used to see which of the three letters to change (first, second, or third). By changing this letter to one of their choosing, students invent a new word. |

For example, if a six is spun, the student is on the space that says *job*. If the second spinner indicates that the third letter is to be changed, the student can make *jot* or *jog*. If the first letter is changed, the new word might be *rob, gob, lob*, etc. If the second letter is changed, the result would be *jab* or *jib*. Nonsense words may be used. At each turn, the students write the word from the game board on a sheet of paper and then write the new word next to it *(job, jot)*. Winners must be able to read their whole list.

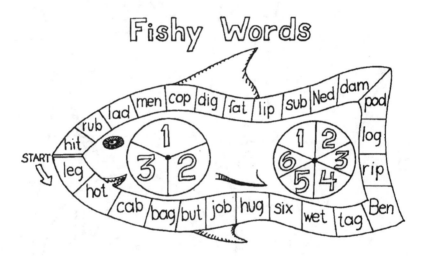

*VARIATIONS:* **Comparatives**

1. The words on the game board might include: big, little, smart, tall, sad, happy, fast, bright, slim, nice, fine, funny, cute, fat, thin, good, careful, bad, naughty, sweet, kind, mean, silly, small, sleepy.
2. Rather than numbers, the second spinner has the following sentences:
   a. She is a _____ girl.
   b. Jack is _____ than Tom.
   c. They are the _____ children in the class.
   3. Students complete the sentences, using the correct form of the adjectives met on the board.

**Multiple Meanings**

1. The spinners used are the ones indicated above (a. 1-6; b. 1-3). The number on the second spinner indicates whether one, two, or three meanings must be provided for the word on the game board at each turn.
2. Appropriate words for the game board include: well, run, light, hand, fire, hit, clear, iron, pen, save, spot, pick, star, note, hail, ball, point, bed, bill, jam, fine, sight, still, bear, hang.

# Fishy Words

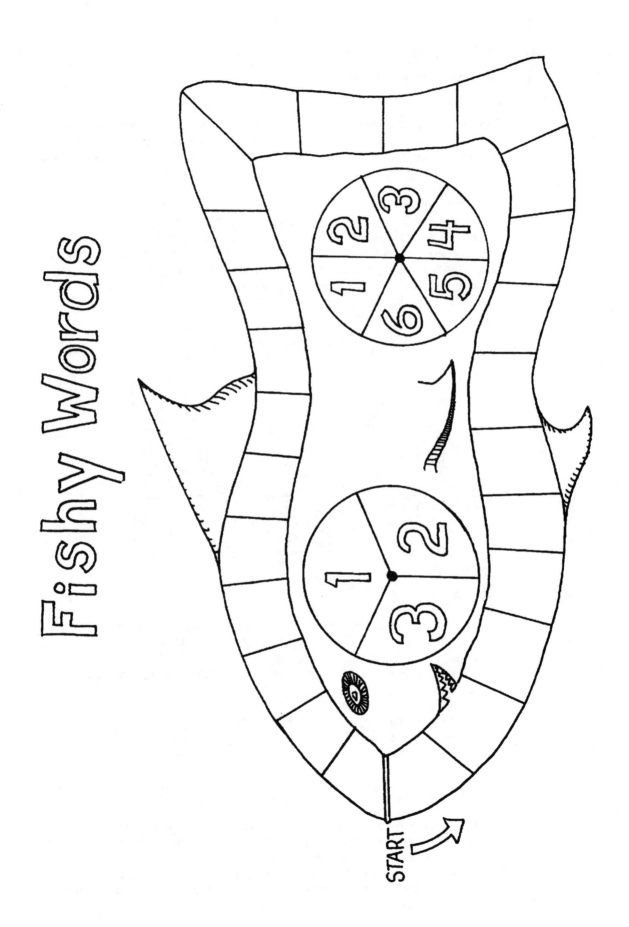

# 3

# Structural Analysis

## DESCRIBING THE SKILL

Many students read quite competently until they encounter a multisyllabic word. Typically, those students look up for help without even attempting to read the word. They need to know that this word can be decoded by dividing it into smaller, more manageable segments. Morphemic and syllabic analysis, components of structural analysis, offer students approaches for accomplishing this.

When students encounter an unknown word that they cannot identify through the context or similarity to a known word, they should be encouraged to look within the word for a recognizable root and its accompanying prefix and/or ending(s). This is morphemic analysis: a concern with the meaningful parts of words—roots, prefixes, and suffixes.

A morpheme may be bound or free. A free morpheme or root word can stand alone. Compound words contain two free morphemes as in *playground*. A bound morpheme, such as the *s* in *boys*, which signals that the noun *boy* is plural, only exists in connection with a free morpheme, in this case the word *boy*. All plurals, as well as derivatives, comparatives, and possessives combine free and bound morphemes (the root word + the affix).

The meaning transmitted by each of the free or bound morphemes in the categories above aids students in reading the resulting words. In the word *walked*, for example, students can identify the *-ed* inflectional ending as a past tense marker. Although the *-ed* marker can be pronounced in three different ways (/ed/, /d/, or /t/ ), students may know the correct pronunciation for the past tense of *walk*, since this word is in their listening-speaking vocabularies. How morphemic analysis helps to build vocabulary is discussed in Chapter 6.

When a multisyllabic word has no affixes, students may need to segment the word in a different way. Students are then encouraged to consider syllabic analysis, the other component of structural analysis. Syllabic analysis deals with a word's structure by dividing the word into its syllables (word segments, each containing one sounded vowel) so that the smaller segments can be more readily identified. Students then blend these segments to produce the word.

When students divide words into syllables, there are two approaches that you may wish to encourage. In the first, the students

1. Identify the phonogram with the first vowel (*car*pet).
2. Add the onset (*car*).
3. With the next vowel, identify the phonogram (et).
4. Add the onset (*pet*).
5. Blend the word.

You may also with to teach students about open or closed syllables with their corresponding vowel sounds.

1.   An open syllable ends in a vowel (CV) and usually produces a long vowel sound. Students can identify the *ri* in *rifle* as a syllable requiring a long sound so that the word is pronounced correctly as *rīfle* rather than *rifle*.
2.   A closed syllable (VC or CVC) ends in a consonant and usually produces a short vowel sound. Although *canteen* may look like an unfamiliar and therefore difficult word, once the word is syllabicated, the two parts *can* and *teen* are easily read.

Because the vowel in an unaccented syllable usually has the *schwa* sound, open and closed syllables are most effective for decoding a stressed syllable, usually the first syllable. This is often enough, however, to get students into the word and with context, facilitate their identifying the word as a whole. Usually generalizations for accenting and an understanding of the *schwa* sound are taught along with generalizations for syllabic analysis. (See "Teaching the Skill" later in this chapter.)

Having said all this, it is important to note that students who are not having special difficulties reading multisyllabic words may not need an emphasis on syllabic analysis for decoding. For most students, this can more often be taught as a writing skill for dividing words at the end of a line. In these cases, the dictionary provides the verification for the generalizations that you may wish to teach your students. (See "Teaching the Skill.")

## IDENTIFYING THE SKILL NEED

As students read aloud, you may wish to provide some instruction in structural analysis if you note some of the following behaviors. It is important to distinguish, however, between nonstandard English usage that may result in omitted endings, and errors that show problems in reading words with inflectional endings. (For a fuller discussion of this topic, refer to Chapter 14.)

*   Some students are uncomfortable reading long words.
*   When reading inflected words, students may forget to use context and consequently read "He jump ed off the box," an error that they would not make if they were attending to the content.
*   Students may be identifying a prefix when in fact the letters do not act as a prefix in the given word (*remnant, unite*). Moreover, they may be looking for little words in big ones (*or* in *word*) rather than looking for root words with prefixes and suffixes or phonograms and onsets.
*   Students may mispronounce certain affixes (*anti*trust, el*a*tion, restive).
*   Accenting the wrong syllable and/or lack of familiarity with the schwa sound can prevent students from recognizing their pronunciation of the word.

## TEACHING THE SKILL: TECHNIQUES AND ACTIVITIES

### SEEING IS BELIEVING

When you are reading to students, stop when you come to multisyllabic words, both with or without affixes, and model how you decode the word. For some words, identify the phonograms and onsets. For inflected or derived words, identify roots and affixes. For multisyllabic roots, use syllabic analysis. Write the word in question on the board, so that students may observe the letters as you describe your approach. When students are reading together in pairs, have them demonstrate to each other how to decode a multisyllabic word.

### GET TO THE ROOT OF THINGS

Before attempting to divide a word into syllables, teach students to look for a recognizable root. *Unreadable* may seem impossible to decode until the student sees the root word *read* and then sees that a prefix and suffix are attached. By looking for roots, students can avoid such errors as treating the *re* in remnant as a prefix.

### TEACH AFFIXES WHEN A ROOT IS LEARNED

When students learn verbs such as *like* and *jump*, teach them *likes, liked, liking, jumps, jumped, jumping* at the same time so that they get used to seeing the root with endings and can recognize it as such. Practice using words with inflectional endings in cloze sentences so that students recognize that context must be used with structural analysis.

*EXAMPLE*    John was _____ up and down.

jumps    jumped    jumping

### LEARN THE COMMON AFFIXES AND THEIR MEANINGS

When you encounter affixed words in reading, use these as an opportunity to plan specific lessons in which you teach common affixes *(re, un, im, in, less, ful, able)*. Show how they are added to a root and change meaning. It is useful for students to know the meaning of some of the more common affixes; awareness of meaning aids word identification as well.

### USE YOUR FINGERS

Have students cover affixes with their fingers as soon as they can spot them. Once they have decoded the root word, the affix is easy to add and the word as a whole seems less difficult.

### SYSTEM ANALYSIS

In a sentence such as "She was unforgettably beautiful," students meet a multisyllabic word composed of a root with a prefix and suffixes. After determining the root, students may find it easier to add the suffixes first and then the prefix.

1. remove the prefix and suffixes: forget
2. decode the root: forget
3. put the suffixes back: forgettably
4. put the prefix back: unforgettably

Students enjoy the security that a reliable system offers.

## BOB'S READING BILL'S BOOKS

Teach the differences between contractions, possessives, and plurals. Many students confuse contractions and possessives because of the apostrophe, and possessives and plurals because of the *s* ending. Help students to understand the meanings of individual contractions. Often students do not relate the printed word to what is commonplace in their oral usage.

Exercises for distinguishing between contractions, possessives, and plurals are easily constructed from the materials children are reading. For the book, *There's a Boy in the Girls' Bathroom* (Sachar, 1987), appropriate exercises might include:

1. Match the underlined word in the following sentence to the correct meaning:
   a. "<u>Bradley's</u> home!" (p. 9)

   Bradley is        more than one Bradley

   b. The pond was a purple stain on *Bradley's* bedspread . . . (p. 11)

   the bedspread of Bradley        Bradley is

   c. "You went into the <u>girls'</u> bathroom?" (p. 35)

   bathroom of the girl        bathroom of the girls

   d. . . . he was at the <u>counselor's</u> office. (p. 31)

   office of the counselor        office of the counselors

2. Choose the correct word for each sentence.
   a. "The _____ the biggest animal . . ." (p. 38)

   elephants        elephant's        elephants'

   b. ". . . if a mouse ran up an _____ trunk . . . (p. 39)

   elephants        elephant's        elephants'

3. Have students write a paragraph explaining the difference between being caught in the girl's bathroom and being caught in the girls' bathroom.

## TEACH SPELLING RULES FOR SUFFIXES

Students often have difficulty with inflected or derived words in which the spelling of the root changes *(hoped or hoping.)* You may feel the need to show students how to add suffixes that begin with a vowel.

1. Double the final consonant for CVC single-syllable words or accented CVC last syllables.

   tap = tapped, tapping
   omit = omitted, omitting

2. Drop the final *e* for VCe words.

   faked, faking, faker

3. Change the *y* to *i*.*

   carried, carrier

Although these generalizations are usually relevant for spelling purposes, students may need to learn them for decoding as well.

## SYLLABLE GENERALIZATIONS

A familiarity with syllable generalizations is useful for end line divisions in writing and can help with decoding as well. In either case, stress that these rules must be used flexibly. If, for example, the V/CV rule doesn't produce a recognizable word, try VC/V. It is important to remember that these generalizations offer students a means of visually segmenting words so that they may then decode only three or four letters at a time. Segmenting words that can already be pronounced is a waste of time. Teach syllabication with *unknown* words.

Here are the generalizations:

1. Every syllable has a sounded vowel. A syllable may have three vowel letters but since two of the vowels are silent, it is still a single syllable (*geese*).
2. Compound words—Divide between the two words.

*EXAMPLE*     play/ground

3. VCCV—When two consonants appear between two sounded vowels, divide between the two consonants. This normally will leave a CVC first syllable that is easy to decode and gives the student a good start on the word. Remember that a consonant digraph and some consonant clusters act as a single letter and relate to the VCV generalization below.

*EXAMPLES*     win/dow          but:     le/thal     a/pron
               VC/CV                     V/CV

4. *Cle*—In words that end in *le*, keep the consonant that precedes the *le* with the *le* syllable. This leaves either an open or closed first syllable with its corresponding long or short vowel sound. This is a good time to illustrate how syllabication aids understanding of which vowel sound to use.

*EXAMPLE*     rifle = rīfle not rĭfle

When the *tle* follows an *s*, the *t* is silent—castle, rustle.

*ck* remains with the first syllable (nick/le)

5. VCV—When one consonant appears between two sounded vowels, first try dividing after the first vowel (pa/per). If the resulting word is not recognizable, try dividing after the consonant (rob/in). The concept of open and

---

*Unless: (1) a vowel precedes the *y*—*player*; (2) the suffix is *ing*—*carrying*. For plurals, the *y* (when preceded by a consonant) changes to *i* and the *es* is added—*penny, pennies.*

closed syllables is reinforced here. Consonant digraphs and certain consonant clusters act as one consonant (le/thal, a/pron).

6. Root words—If a word has an affix (prefix and/or suffix or inflectional ending), divide between the root and the affix.

*EXAMPLES*    re/write    un/like/ly

7. Inflectional endings—As a past tense ending, *ed* forms a separate syllable only when it is added to a root word that ends in a *d* or a *t* (plant/ed    need/ed).

When *ion* is added to a word ending in *t, tion* becomes a syllable.

*EXAMPLE*    elect    elec/tion

8. Double vowels—Sometimes double vowels do not form digraphs or diphthongs but are read separately, forming two syllables.

*EXAMPLES*    di/et,    du/et,    nu/cle/us,    ra/di/o,    cre/ate,    o/a/sis

## CONCENTRATE ON THE FIRST SYLLABLE

Help students to see that the first phonogram or syllable of a root word usually results in a CVC or CV configuration and is easily decoded. If students can read the first syllable, this is often enough to give them the confidence to proceed with the word. The context provides additional help.

You may wish to compose cloze sentences, using the first syllable of a difficult word for the deleted word, to illustrate the usefulness of the initial syllable, plus context.

*EXAMPLE*    Tom needed to prac____ his math.

(practice)

Continue by doing the same with a book students are reading. In *The Day We Met You* (Koehler, 1990), you might use the sentences: We bor____ a car seat so you could ride home safe. (p. 5). We bought bottles and for ____ so you wouldn't be hun____ . (p. 7)

## DECODE ONE SYLLABLE AT A TIME

Sometimes it helps students to overcome their fear of long words by isolating the first syllable and then covering the rest of the word with a finger. Four letters at a time is "do-able" when the whole word is formidable.

## USE MOST COMMON ACCENT GENERALIZATIONS

Help students to understand stress or accent. Show them that:

1. Most two-syllable words have the stress on the first syllable unless the second syllable has a long vowel sound.

*EXAMPLE*    car´ pet    com plain´

2. Root words are usually accented rather than their affixes.

*EXAMPLE*     un hap´ py      care´ ful

3.  The syllable before the syllable *tion* is often an open syllable with a long sound and is accented.

*EXAMPLE*     re la´ tion     sol u´ tion     com mo´ tion

## SCHWA

Teach students about the schwa sound (this usually sounds quite like the short *u* sound */uh/—a agree*, but sometimes may sound like short *e* or *i*—*de cide*—depending on an individual's dialect). It is especially confusing with syllables like *age* (usage), *ite* (composite), *ive* (explosive) where the silent *e* leads students to expect that the preceding vowel will be long. Because the syllable is unaccented, the vowel produces the schwa rather than the long sound. The schwa sound appears in most unaccented syllables.

## PROVIDE LOTS OF PRACTICE

Examples of practice techniques may include card games. The words can come from the books your students are reading. Perhaps a card taped to the inside cover of a book will alert students that a card game is available for this book.

1.  *Concentration*—Pairs could include contraction and meaning (we've/we have), root and derivative (do/undo), two syllables that comprise a word (sta/tion), etc.
2.  *Calling All Cards*—Using fifty-two cards, thirteen packs of four cards each are created. On each of the four cards in a pack, have the students write a verb and each of its three inflections, underlining a different tense each time.

| <u>jump</u> | jump | jump | jump |
| jumps | <u>jumps</u> | jumps | jumps |
| jumped | jumped | <u>jumped</u> | jumped |
| jumping | jumping | jumping | <u>jumping</u> |

Procedure: Three or more may play. Each player is dealt four cards and the remainder of the pack is placed face down. The first player looks at one of his cards and asks for a word on the card which is not underlined on that card or any of his cards. If he gets it, he may ask again. Otherwise, he draws from the remaining deck. When four cards of a book have been completed, the book is placed on the table. The player with the most books wins.

# Activities to Go

**Can You Strike 100?**

SKILL: Syllabication

MATERIAL: Game board, pen or pencil

PROCEDURE:
1. Fill in the game board with syllables as shown below.
2. Student pronounces the three syllables on each bowling pin, unscrambles them, and then writes the whole word on the line provided.
3. Each correct word is worth ten points.

   Extra three syllable words: *invention, reproduce, unbutton, position, recognize, crocodile, episode, saxophone, satisfy, comical.*

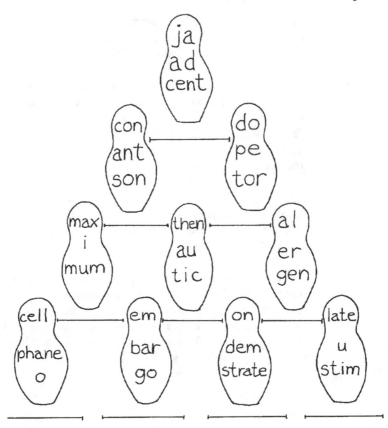

CAN YOU STRIKE 100 ?

VARIATION: Long and short vowel words: On each pin write a vowel symbol (for example, a). Then write two words. Student copies the word which matches the symbol, writing it on the line provided.

| | | |
|---|---|---|
| ă—scratch, pain | ĕ—then, three | ĭ—kilt, kind |
| ŏ—clock, cloak | ŭ—cub, cube | ă—strap, stray |
| ē—treat, threat | ī—site, gift | ō—blond, boast |
| ū—fuse, fuss | | |

# CAN YOU STRIKE 100 ?

NAME: **Rerouted**

SKILL: Structural analysis

MATERIALS: Game board, pencil

PROCEDURE: 1. Students find and mark the open route through the maze, one in which only derived or inflected words are found (those with an affix). Each word students encounter, they must read. If a word isn't affixed, students must try another route.

2. The seven nonaffixed words are distractors—they look like derived words but they are only roots: *digest, remnant, presto, talent, jackal, unite, disco.* These words block maze paths and the students, when encountering one, must reroute.

# REROUTED

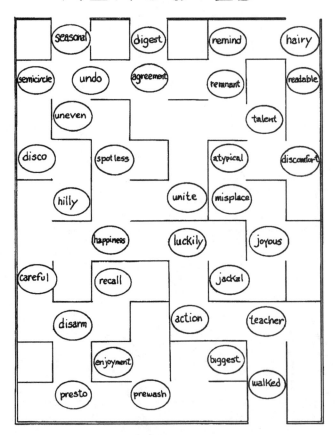

VARIATIONS: **a.** Word meanings: students find the route where all words are related in meaning. Related words: say, talk, exclaim, shout, whisper, speak, remark, ask, nag, call, state, utter, tell, relate, express, chatter, answer, beg, announce, voice, stutter, claim, suggest, plead, reply

Distractors: friend, seven, arrive, who, sense, chapter, want

**b.** Phonics: Twenty-five short or long vowel words may be used with seven distractors containing other vowel sounds.

# REROUTED

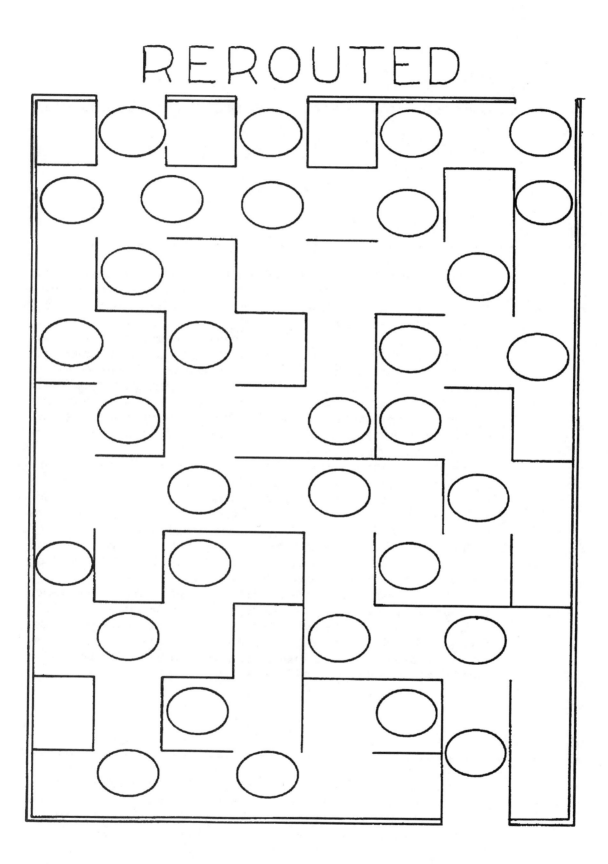

43

# 4

# Contextual Analysis

Although students may need to be taught to use the clues in written context to identify unknown words, they are continually processing context cues in spoken language. Use of context is, therefore, a familiar skill and can be used as an aid to identify words in reading from the start.

For able readers, contextual analysis is a skill in constant use. Capable readers predict and then accept or reject word identification on the basis of whether or not the word fits the sense of the sentence. Selecting from the available cues, readers use their experiences with and understandings about language to make predictions.

Contextual analysis requires readers to attend to the whole sentence or text in order to identify an unknown word within it. As readers use the context, they may be given numbers of cues. These cues can be semantic (meaning), syntactic (grammatical), and/or pictorial (nonverbal).

Reading depends on the interaction between word identification and meaning. When readers identify words or verify their predictions, an interaction takes place between contextual (meaning, grammar, pictures) cues and letters. The importance given to any one cue is always a relational one and dependent on the particular sentence. For example, the omitted word in "She read the _____" is limited syntactically to a noun and semantically to something that can be read (book, note, paper, newspaper, etc.). The beginning and ending letters $p$ and $r$ narrow the choices still further. The word *paper* is the logical choice.

Contextual analysis has yet two other roles. In addition to assisting unknown word identification as described above, contextual analysis aids in determining correct pronunciation or stress for certain words (*read, read, object, object*). It also plays an active role in vocabulary building, often providing meanings for new words or alternate meetings for known words. For further discussion of this last aspect of contextual analysis, see Chapter 6.

## IDENTIFYING THE SKILL NEED

As you listen to students read, you may note various reading behaviors that suggest that instruction in contextual analysis might be beneficial.

When an unfamiliar word appears at the beginning or middle of a sentence, many students "stop dead" as they seek help, rather than continuing on to see if the rest of the sentence aids in identifying the unknown word.

Others may read through a sentence where the unknown word appears at the end and still look for help or they may supply an inaccurate word, failing in either case to utilize available context.

When students supply a word that is incorrect, often it is because they are focusing on only one aspect of the context.

For example, in the sentence "The walls were painted red," students who read: "The walls were bright red" are attending to meaning—the sentence makes sense— but they are ignoring the letters.

*A CAUTION*  It is important to recognize that sometimes students are unable to take advantage of the contextual clues because they lack the background knowledge that the text calls for either in terms of concepts or vocabulary. With more familiar subject matter, these students might utilize context clues appropriately.

## TEACHING THE SKILL: TECHNIQUES AND ACTIVITIES

### SHARED READING PROMOTES USE OF CONTEXT

The kinds of books that are appropriate for a shared reading experience (Chapter 1: Sight Vocabulary) help students to anticipate what the words will say by their emphasis on predictable text, rhyme, and repetition. Students in classrooms who read numbers of books in this fashion are learning to pay attention to context.

### SPOKEN LANGUAGE DEMONSTRATES THE USE OF CONTEXT

Show students how context helps them to anticipate what an unknown word might be. Omit a word in a sentence spoken orally and ask the students to supply the missing word. Using a very predictable word for the omission helps make the point.

Examples of appropriate sentences might be:

Please pass the salt and _____ .

The boy at bat hit a home _____ .

The child likes to _____ rope.

We _____ in a house.

### MOVE FROM USE OF SPOKEN LANGUAGE TO WRITTEN LANGUAGE

Explain that exactly the same process used above is at work in determining what an unknown word is in a reading selection. With spoken language, the word was omitted; with written language, the word is unknown. It's as if it were omitted.

a.  Write a sentence on the board with an easy word omitted. (The boy read the

_____ .)

b.  Brainstorm possibilities with the students and write the words on the board. (book, sign, magazine, newspaper, etc.)

c.  Write the sentence with the first letter of the word written or the first and

last letters written. (The boy read the b____k.)

d.  Write the sentence with the whole word. (The boy read the book.)

e. Repeat the procedure, this time using a difficult, unknown word. (The boy read the <u>newspaper</u>.)
f. Demonstrate this process in a book by covering words that are easily predicted. Show the students that they can guess what the word will be. Remove the covering slowly from the left, revealing a letter at a time to confirm the guesses. Big Books with their predictable text are appropriate materials to use.

### DON'T STOP

Difficult words appearing at the end of a sentence are the easiest to identify when using context. For unknown words that appear at the beginning or in the middle of a sentence, be sure to have the students read the entire sentence before attempting the word.

*EXAMPLE* The *raft* was made of wood so it would float.

Sometimes the sentences before and after must also be read.

*EXAMPLE* The boy watched the *parade*. First came the bands, then the floats, and then the clowns.

### HERE'S HOW

Have students substitute a silly word for every unknown word. The students might read, "In the kazoom *(parade)*, there were bands, floats, clowns, and marchers." By substituting a word, students may continue with the sentence without losing continuity of thought. They may then go back and fill in the appropriate word if the context has enabled them to think of a word that both fits the sense of the sentence and the letters shown.

### STRESS STRESS—PRONUNCIATION TOO

To determine appropriate pronunciation or stress, students should read the whole sentence. Some words can only be identified in context—words like "live," "refuse." Always teach the two pronunciations from the start and illustrate how only context can help the student to know which word is being used.
Examples of other ambiguous words:

1. Vowel change: *read, lead, bow, sow, wind, wound, tear.*
2. Stress change: *object, present, rebel, conduct, permit, record, digest, escort, annex, combat.*

### UNDERSTANDING WHY

Omit words in written sentences (The cat _____ the milk quickly. I read a good _____ today.) or use nonsense words instead of blanks. When asking the students to supply possibilities for the missing or nonsense word in each sentence, discuss with them how they came up with these choices. What helped them? By verbalizing what they are doing, they will become more aware of how context is used and what factors (syntax, meaning, letters, word length) must be satisfied.

EXAMPLES       We ate at our new seppin and chairs.
               We should walk and not lub in the halls.
               The car stopped at the blag light.

## COVERING UP

It often helps to have students cover the unknown word with their fingers and try to think of an appropriate word before seeing whether the letter and word length cues fit. Too much information to deal with at one time may be overwhelming for some students.

## WHAT DO YOU KNOW?

When assigning reading, be sure that you do not skip the prereading discussion. Familiarize students with the words and concepts they'll be meeting before they begin the reading. By doing this, you will help to establish appropriate expectations and maximize potential use of context clues.

a.   Have students brainstorm words they believe may appear in the text and check to see how many actually do.
b.   Word maps are a graphic means of highlighting a concept. As students supply words relevant to the concept, they develop—through discussion—background knowledge and vocabulary that will enable them to use context clues more easily if needed. See page 65.

## BEGIN AGAIN

When students try an unknown word in oral reading and substitute a non-meaningful pronunciation, urge them to start the sentence again, or repeat the preceding one to two sentences to get into the "swing" of meaning and thus utilize available context clues. When a self-correction occurs from this process, liberal praise for students is suggested.

**NAME:** **Filling In**

**SKILL:** Contextual analysis

**MATERIALS:** Game board, twelve game cards

**PROCEDURE:**
1. On each of twelve cards write a skill sentence (see below).
2. Lay out the game cards with the skill sentences face down. On the side facing up, number the cards from 1 to 12 so that the numbers are showing.
3. Have the students proceed along the board space by space, clockwise, choosing which cards to read by figuring out the arithmetic problem in each space. For example, the starting space (10 + 1) = 11. Therefore, the card 11 will be turned over and read.
4. If students can get through the board with no mistakes, they are SUPER, 1 to 2 mistakes = GOOD, 3 to 5 = FAIR.

There are different ways to write the skill sentences for the card, as shown in the examples for sentence 1.

*Skill Sentences for Cards*

1. The dog's _____ is Spot.*
2. He _____ the house white.
3. She wants _____ come, too.
4. She had a big _____ on her face.
5. _____ like to eat.
6. The _____ was beautiful.
7. What _____ did you come home?
8. He picked the lovely _____ .
9. Did you _____ that book yet?
10. He _____ the house today.
11. She _____ to school.
12. He felt _____ from eating that candy.

*Example: A card might follow any of the following patterns:

The dog's _____ is Spot.
The dog's n_____ is Spot.
The dog's n_____e is Spot.
The dog's n_m_ is Spot.
The dog's _ _ _ _ is Spot.

**VARIATIONS:** Almost every skill can be used with this board. Twelve cards are made with the words or sentences to be practiced. A combination of skills may also be used. Examples:

a. Consonant clusters: pot, spot    rave, grave    sin, skin   etc.
b. Twelve sight word demons: their   who   want,   etc.
c. Twelve words underlined in sentences with two or three definitions given on the following page. Students identify the correct one.

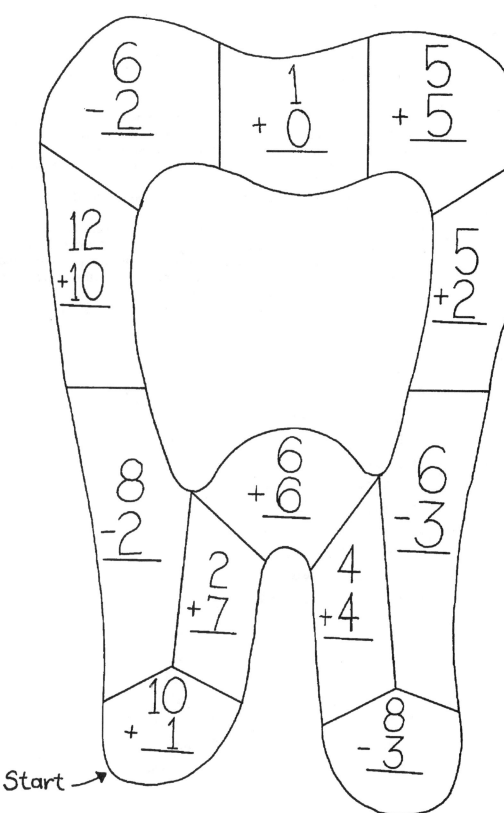

**Concentrate**

Contextual analysis

MATERIALS: Game board, eleven pairs of word (word and sentence) cards

PROCEDURE: Students play "Concentration"

1. Eleven pairs of cards are made. On one card of each pair, write a sentence with a word missing. In the suggested sentences below, the missing word appears at the end, beginning, or middle of sentences and represents different parts of speech (noun, verb, etc.). For the matching eleven cards use the eleven words that complete the sentence.
2. The 22 cards are placed face down, one in each box on the board, covering the numbers.
3. The first player turns over two cards. If the two cards picked are a pair—that is, if the sentence can be completed sensibly by the word turned over—the player marks down the total number of points given in each box uncovered, keeps the pair, and takes another turn. If the cards do not form a pair, they are turned back over and the next player continues.
4. The winner can be the player with the most points or the most pairs.

*Sentence Cards:*

1. The ice cubes _____ in the sun.
2. That is _____ car.
3. _____ did you go?
4. The book was _____ two other books.
5. Her hair looked _____ .
6. He walked away _____ .
7. She will _____ the letter.
8. She needed to buy food at the _____ .
9. Put away your _____ !
10. _____ came to the party.
11. He was _____ the baby.

*Word Cards:*

1. melted
2. their
3. where
4. between
5. beautiful
6. slowly

7. write
8. market
9. clothes
10. they
11. carrying

*VARIATIONS:* This game may be used wherever pairs of cards are suitable.

a. Word pairs with matching sounds—cat, sad; key, seal; made, rain; comb, soap; etc.
b. Homonyms—here, hear; die, dye; there, their; break, brake; etc.
c. Words with the same roots—review, viewing; unhappy, happily; replay, playful; misread, readable; etc.
d. Compound words or contractions—base, ball; did not, didn't; I'll, I will; play, ground; etc.
e. Synonyms or antonyms—malign (slander, praise); lucid (clear, cloudy); See words under TIC TACKY TOE (see Chapter 8, "Activities to Go").
f. Sight words—Eleven pairs of sight words or sight phrases must be created.
g. Inferences—Sentences using figurative language and sentences or phrases with the same meaning: "He was in the doghouse with his parents"; "His parents were angry with him," etc.

# CONCENTRATE

| 9 | 8 | 3 | 7 | 2 |
|---|---|---|---|---|
| 7 | | | | 4 |
| 4 | | SCORE | | 1 |
| 2 | | PLAYER·1 \| PLAYER·2 | | 5 |
| 5 | | | | 6 |
| 3 | | | | 7 |
| 6 | 8 | 2 | 4 | 1 |

# 5

# Concepts about Print

## DESCRIBING THE SKILL

"Concepts about print" refers to special skills and strategies that are necessary to understand the conventions of print and the mechanics of reading. Students need to know that (1) oral and written language can be broken into units called words, (2) spoken words can be divided into syllables and sounds, which can then be blended back into words, (3) written words are composed of letters, (4) both individual written words and lines of print are scanned from left to right, and (5) lines of print are read from top to bottom. These skills are part of learning to read and write.

Other concepts about print are concerned with the terminology of reading instruction. Directions in workbooks often include terms like *beginning letter, matching sound,* and *next to.* Without knowledge of the meanings of these terms, students may have difficulty learning to read the way it is taught in school. In addition, terms that describe the conventions of print such as *capital letter, quotation marks,* and *period* require special instructional attention.

Concepts about print are often acquired through informal preschool exposure, such as parent read-alouds or shared reading experiences. Some students, though, lack such exposure, and still others require direct, formal instruction in the skills.

Direct instruction in these concepts is sometimes neglected in classrooms. Even though you may model left-to-right processing when you read with students from the chalkboard or a Big Book, students also need guidance with left-to-right scanning through directed practice.

## IDENTIFYING THE SKILL NEED

Perhaps the most practical way to assess students' concepts about print is through observation. Shared reading or writing affords many opportunities to observe students' use of directionality and word sense. The best time to observe students' sound and syllabication abilities may be during phonics instruction and through analyzing invented spellings in their written work. Assessing students' knowledge of instructional language can take place during all kinds of instruction, but can be assessed most effectively during workbook or worksheet lessons.

In addition to observation, certain informal assessments may be useful. Asking students to point to the first letter of a word and then the first word in a sentence will show something of their segmentation abilities with written language. Similarly, asking them to repeat the first sound in a word and then the first word in a sentence will show something of their segmentation abilities with spoken language.

Standardized reading assessments are not particularly useful for assessing abilities in print concepts, primarily because they are group tests and an individual student's strategies for approaching print cannot be evaluated. Individually administered tests, however, can be useful. A diagnostic reading test, an informal reading inventory, or a running record can include observations about a student's concepts about print.

## TEACHING THE SKILLS: TECHNIQUES AND ACTIVITIES

### ORIENTATION TO PRINT

**Green Means Go**
Modify texts in any or all of the following ways so that students will be signaled to begin reading each line of print and each word at the left side and progress through it to the right: (1) color the first letter of each word green, (2) use a green vertical line at the beginning of each line of text, (3) number the words in the order in which they are to be read, (4) number the letters of a word in the order in which they are to be decoded, and (5) use left-to-right arrows underneath a line of print. It is important to fade gradually whichever cues are used so that students don't use the cues as crutches.

**Left, Right**
When reading words from the board or from text that students can also see, you can sweep your hand or finger underneath words and phrases as you pronounce them. Big Books are particularly suited to this kind of modeling. When writing, make sure that students can see each word or line revealed from left to right. Allowing students to use their fingers or a marker as a beginning step is helpful.

**Start at the Beginning**
For students with left–right orientation problems, certain methods of word analysis can compound their reading difficulties. For example, urging such students to decode a word from the vowel to the final consonant and then to attach the initial consonant (*a-t, c-a-t, cat*) or through identification of graphemic base first (*-at, cat*) may disrupt their shaky hold on left-to-right word processing. Likewise, a search for a word's root may cause these students to start reading in the middle of a word.

Better word-processing techniques for these students would be left-to-right phonic or structural analysis, kinesthetic techniques where students trace the letters of a word as it is decoded, and the use of tachistoscopes, devices that frame a word or phrase and reveal a little of it at a time in a left-to-right progression.

### WORD AND LETTER CONSCIOUSNESS

**Marking a Text**
You or your students can mark a photocopied text. Words or letters can be circled, underlined, or X'ed, and then counted. To lend variety to this activity, try putting boxes around the words and letters of large-size print and then using the boxes to guide cutting the text into individual words and letters.

### Carefully Prepared Materials

If letter and word boundaries are not clearly delineated in materials you make, or on the chalkboard, students may have difficulty reading. Care needs to be taken to space letters so none touch. For example, when *c* and *l* are printed close together, they look like a *d*. Leaving even-sized spaces between words is also important. (Always remember the difference between *a gain* and *again!*)

### Word Searches

The task in a word search is to separate a group of letters that make a word from a group of random letters. Word search puzzles are found everywhere, from airline magazines to the daily newspaper. Some of them, however, embed words vertically, diagonally, and backwards. For most students, it makes sense to design teacher-made word searches that embed words from left to right only.

A variation on word searches is word tracking. It requires students to find and mark a specific word in a field of distractors that may look similar or have a related meaning.

*EXAMPLE*   Find *cookie:*

> *shook crook cookie cook*
> *cake cookie cracker jam pie cookie*
> *cookie ice cream tart cookie pudding*

### What's a Word?

To help students distinguish between letters and words, have them circle the letters and underline the words. Explain how *I* and *a* fit in both categories or omit them from your exercise.

*EXAMPLE*      *b     be     only     on     a*

Circle *b*, underline *be, only, on,*
   circle and underline *a*

In later exercises, real words can be contrasted with letter clusters and then with nonsense words.

### Labeling

Putting labels on a selected number of objects in a room, on bulletin boards, and on job charts helps students learn that one word equals one thing or concept. To make this technique effective, overlabeling should be avoided. Also, the words should be used in language arts activities and seen frequently in other meaningful contexts, such as stories and signs.

### Cut and Match

Have students cut apart familiar words into individual letters and familiar sentences into individual words. They can then reassemble the words and sentences. Students may also enjoy selecting and then cutting out written words that have the same first letter as a target letter that you show them.

### Voice Pointing

For this technique, students point to each word in a memorized story as they read it aloud. It allows them to learn what the words they are saying from memory look like. It also encourages awareness of the spaces between words.

You may want to voice point when you read aloud, especially from a Big Book. A pointer or a finger are both fine for the purpose. You may want to point above the word so as not to obscure the text in the next line of print.

**Language Experience Approach**
Showing students that what they say can be written is recommended to increase their written word and left-to-right concepts. To maximize attention to these concepts when using the approach: (1) say each word as you print it, (2) point to each word as you read the entire story, (3) point to each word as children read the story, (4) identify words that appear more than once, (5) count all the words in the story, pointing as you go, and then let children count them, (6) count letters within some of the words, and (7) find some words that begin with the same letter.

## INSTRUCTIONAL TERMINOLOGY

**Listen Carefully**
Depending on the age of your students, a number of oral language activities use reading terminology. For primary grade students, the records of Hap Palmer or Ella Jenkins provide songs that require physical response based on oral directions. For somewhat older students, the familiar song and dance The Hokey Pokey, and the game Simple Simon may be helpful. Another favorite is Hot and Cold, a game in which students search for a hidden object, as you provide them with hints ("a little more to the left," "look below the table").

**Circle, Underline, Cross Out**
Some of the key terms used during reading instruction are:

| | | | |
|---|---|---|---|
| *circle* | *before* | *letter* | *end* |
| *underline* | *after* | *sound* | *then* |
| *cross out* | *word* | *first* | *alike* |
| *above* | *below* | *over* | *under* |
| *next to* | *beside* | *same* | *different* |

Attention to these terms can help students better understand the special conventions of print. For example, a lesson in *same* and *different* could focus on how words are the same only when the letters are the same and in the same order—even when they are written in different typefaces. GUM, gum, gum, and **gum** are the same, while *gym* and *mug* are different from *gum*.

**Punk-chew-a-shun**
Translate the visuals of punctuation (. , ? ! " ") into a code that communicates some of the meaning behind these symbols. When reading aloud from a text that students can see, you might want to say "Stop" at a period and "Slow" at a comma. You might say "Question" at a question mark, "Wow" at an exclamation mark, and "Look who's talking" at quotation marks. Your students may enjoy creating their own classroom code.

## PHONEMIC AWARENESS

The object of the following recommendations is to raise students' consciousness about how words can be separated auditorially into parts.

### Divide and Conquer

Give students experience with auditory analysis and synthesis. With them, take words apart orally and put them back together. You can do this with syllables (*splin-ter, splinter*), cluster by graphemic base (*spl-int, splint*), chunk by chunk (*spl-in-ter* or *spl-int-er, splinter*), or phoneme by phoneme (*s-p-l-i-n-t-e-r, splinter*).

### Count the Sounds

Have students count the sounds in the words you say. Start with words with two sounds, such as *I'm, at, up,* and *out,* and then progress to words with more sounds as students are ready. You may want to have them put blocks or other small objects out to represent the number of sounds they hear, such as three blocks for *cat* and four for *crash*.

### Guess the Word

Riddles with both a meaning cue and the first syllable or sound encourage children to think about and use word parts.

EXAMPLES

I'm thinking of a word that rhymes with glove and means "push."
Which word starts with /p/ and means "water on the sidewalk after it rains?"
Guess this word—it means "short coat" and starts with "jac."

### Antidisestablishmentarianism

Students' interest in the sounds or parts of words can be engaged by unusual language—rhymes, alliteration, the "pows" and "tee-hees" of comic books, and by long unknown or nonsense words (*supercalifragilisticexpealidotious*). Interesting words are found in literature by Dr. Seuss and William Steig.

### Get the Beat

Start with easily separable or syncopated rhythms so that students can tap out the beat with percussion instruments or with a pencil on their desks. This will be the only time that this activity is sanctioned in school! Move on to rhythmic poetry and songs.

### Collage It

Help students to make a classroom collage using cut out magazine pictures that start with a particular letter or end with a target rhyme pattern. Label the collage with the letter and, if you wish, label the pictures, underlining the key letter(s).

# Activities to Go

NAME: **A Day in School**

SKILL: Instructional vocabulary

MATERIALS: Picture and cut-out

PROCEDURE: 1. Students will use the cut-out below to follow the oral directions.
2. You may choose from the following phrases or write your own.
Directions:

Place _____ (a name that students choose for the cut-out):

> to the left of the blackboard
> in front of the teacher's desk
> at the bottom of the room
> beside the door
> below the flag
> next to the bookshelf
> under the bulletin board
> to the right of Sally's desk
> above the window

Let _____ go to the chalkboard and:

> underline the word *brown*
> point to the first letter in the sentence
> circle the last word in the sentence
> put a box around the letter at the end of *fox*
> find the two words in the sentence that are the same
> cross out the animal words in the sentence
> tell which word comes after *jumped*
> put a line under the first letter in *dog*
> show how the words *fox* and *dog* are the same
> show how the words *fox* and *dog* are different

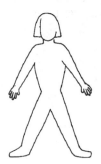

VARIATIONS: Instead of using the Day in School picture, cut out magazine advertisements with interest settings and characters.

Have students give their own directions to the cut-out.

For help with the comprehension skill following directions, have students read the directions instead of listening to them.

# DAY IN SCHOOL

The quick brown fox jumps over the lazy dog.

SALLY'S DESK

NAME: **Walking the Dog**

SKILL: Word tracking

MATERIALS: Game board

PROCEDURE: Students will move the dog cutout through the winding street and have the dog "sniff" each word and bark only when it sniffs the word *dog*.

VARIATIONS: For practice with instructional terminology, print words that start with *d* along with words that start with other letters. Tell students to have the dog bark only when it sniffs a *d* at the beginning of a word. You may want to do the same thing with words that end with *g* or that have *o* in the middle to provide practice with end or final and middle.

For practice with letter consciousness, print words of varying length on the street. Have students move the dog along the street, sniff each word, and bark once for each letter in the word. A three-letter word gets three barks, for example.

# WALKING THE DOG

doggie

dog

DOGE

dig

DOG

bog

pbo

Dog

DOGG

dog

# 6

## Meaning Vocabulary

A good reader is skilled in both word identification and in comprehension. Central to each is a well-developed meaning vocabulary. When students' attempts at pronunciation do not produce a word that they have heard before, their ability to identify words can be affected adversely. Similarly, understanding an author's message is difficult when much of the vocabulary used conveys little or no meaning to students.

Often the meaning of a passage is distorted if students know only one meaning for a word when another is indicated. And it is the more common words that tend to have the most meanings (examples: *run, point, light*). Moreover, knowing that a word has multiple meanings is not always enough. Can readers discern from the text which meaning is intended? Commonly, students tend to focus on the meaning they know best. For example, in the sentence "He saw the bird *light* on the tree before flying away," if students define light as a type of lamp, the sentence will not make sense.

Knowledge of multiple meanings also involves a consideration of connotation and denotation. A word *denotes* a specific meaning or a number of specific meanings that can be found in a dictionary. Words also *connote* meanings, however, which may vary from person to person. Connotations reflect emotions and experiences. Whereas the word *family* connotes warmth and happiness to many of us, to others it may connote strife and anger. Readers, therefore, need exposure to varieties of experiences to comprehend both a word's denotation and its connotation.

Complicating the issue further are the slight variations of meaning that context helps the reader to identify. Words rarely have precise meanings. Their definitions and synonyms reflect their context. The definition of a word in isolation is altered somewhat when the word is put into a sentence or paragraph. When reading "The boy was faced with a *problem*," the decision as to whether this is a simple or complex predicament can only be clarified by the surrounding context.

Students possess four different vocabularies: listening, speaking, reading, and writing, which normally develop in that order. Although at first students' listening vocabularies exceed all others, good readers find that their reading vocabulary eventually outdistances the other three. Listening and reading are receptive skills. These vocabularies tend to be easier to measure and are more representative of word knowledge than the vocabulary evidenced by speaking or writing, the expressive modes. Many of us recognize the meanings of hundreds of words in print that we have never attempted to use. When students use vocabulary, however, either through speaking or writing, competence in the receptive skills is assumed and reinforced.

Vocabulary builds most rapidly when words are met often and in varying circumstances. A papier-maché figure is strengthened by pasting layer upon layer of paper stripping. A single layer of stripping is far too fragile and will not last. Each time students encounter a word, they add another layer to the word's meaning foundation.

## IDENTIFYING THE SKILL NEED

All students need to develop their meaning vocabularies. The more exposure to new words and concepts students receive, the deeper their comprehension of written material will be. Providing experiences to build meaning vocabulary should be a priority of all teachers at all levels.

The reasons for assessing students' vocabularies are varied. Students with wide and varied meaning vocabularies may be capable of reading more challenging material than that currently offered in the classroom. Students with comprehension difficulties may be having problems because they lack the appropriate concepts to understand grade level material.

Certain observations that you make during class discussions may signal a need for bolstering particular vocabulary skills. You may find that some students' experiences may be limited, thereby affecting their exposure to the concepts that prompt language. A wonderful example is the child who, riding in the country for the first time, looks out of the car window at a barn and says "Oh, there's the pancake house." Perhaps this child knew about farms and barns from books, but his primary experience was with a pancake restaurant that was shaped like a barn.

Students who react literally to language may not be recognizing when a word is part of a figurative expression. "Get off my back," Kim shouted. "But I wasn't on your back," Fred whined. "I'm standing right here."

Some students may exhibit problems with homophones (words that sound alike but have different spelling and meaning—*blue, blew*) and homographs (words that look alike but are pronounced differently and have different meanings—wound[oo], wound[ow]).

Students may not be using context to assist in comprehending meaning even when a sentence is contextually rich. Sometimes they are able to use certain contextual cues but not others. For example, students reading "John was loquacious, talkative" might understand the meaning of loquacious. Meeting that word in the sentence "Although John was loquacious, his brother hardly said a word," students might not take note of the signal word *although,* which indicates contrast.

If they are unfamiliar with meanings for morphemes (roots and affixes), they may have trouble using context to reveal meanings of derived words.

EXAMPLE    In a story about a newspaper, a sentence might read, "The *rewrite* man gathered his notes."

Using the prefix *re,* which means "again," the meaning of the unfamiliar word is more easily uncovered.

## TEACHING MEANING VOCABULARY: TECHNIQUES AND ACTIVITIES

Techniques for building meaning vocabulary generally expand students' listening–speaking vocabularies and improve their use of context to discern meaning.

Regardless of how the words are introduced or encountered, an effective means of promoting retention after students have discussed the word with its various meanings and used the word orally, might be to:

1.  Write the word in a personal dictionary, following it either with a picture, a definition, a synonym, or a sentence that utilizes it. Their dictionaries may include words that students want to refer to for either meaning and/or spelling assistance.
2.  Practice using the word:
    a.  In expressive activities such as drama, conversation, and composition.
    b.  In a crossword puzzle or word search or in a game format like Concentration that matches word and definition (or synonym or cloze sentence). Other choices might be bingo games in which synonyms for words read are covered, or dice games in which words might appear on each die. When a die is spun, students must use the word in a sentence to receive points.

## SUGGESTIONS FOR EXPANDING LISTENING–SPEAKING VOCABULARIES

**Reading to Students**

Reading aloud to students cannot be stressed enough as an essential means of introducing students to words. Not only are words used in differing contexts but often slight nuances of meaning are conveyed naturally.

Reading aloud to your less able readers is especially important. These students lack the tools to benefit from the exposure to language and concepts that is accessible to good readers. Hence they find themselves in a bind. Because reading is difficult for these students, they are unlikely to elect it as a leisure activity. Even should they choose to read, the complexity and amount of vocabulary they meet is necessarily limited by the level of the books they are capable of reading. They are therefore prevented from learning new concepts through reading. Moreover, oral language exposure cannot be a substitute, because the sophisticated sentence structure and language usage found in written language rarely occurs in speech.

By reading aloud to students daily, you can help to provide your less avid readers with the vocabulary they are not attaining on their own. The discussion that follows an oral reading should incorporate some of the new concepts or vocabulary. By varying the genre of the material you chose (novels, poetry, biographies, essays, news articles, scientific findings), exposure is increased.

**Go and Do**

Most students learn best by doing. Therefore, first-hand experiences are invaluable vocabulary builders. Students who watch a cow chewing on grass and then get to participate in the milking process, understand *cud* and *udder* far better when these words are used or explained than if they had simply heard you define the words. A student, reading Hal Borland's *When the Legends Die*, brought far greater understanding and appreciation and excitement to her reading after having been to the West, where she saw the lodge pole pines so vividly described in the book.

Take students on field trips, bring experiences to the classroom, and talk. First-hand experience is not always possible in a classroom, but pictures, models, or films act as appropriate backup. As noted in Chapter 1, use of more than one sense enhances memory. A corollary to all of the above is, do not spend your whole day on reading instruction and math, thereby eliminating social studies, science, art, and music from the curriculum. Cross-curricula activities promote a great deal of concept building, which can only enhance reading abilities.

### What Do You Like?
Utilize areas of interest as a focus for developing vocabulary. An interest in biking, for example, might generate from the books students are reading, words such as *gears, axle, accelerate, decelerate, spoke,* and *incline.* Multiple meanings could be a part of any discussion of special interest words. Charts listing words developed around a theme might result and be displayed with words regularly added.

### Preview Vocabulary
Most teacher's manuals that accompany basal and other reading material recommend that vocabulary be previewed before reading a selection. We agree. Preteaching is done to facilitate both understanding of word meaning and word identification. Use this opportunity to expand on the words by discussing: (1) synonyms and antonyms, (2) multiple meanings, and (3) other words utilizing the same root.

### Zero In on Meaning
There are numbers of ways to help students recognize the multiple denotative and connotative aspects to every word. Below are a few suggestions:

1.  *Semantic Mapping*—A stimulus word is chosen. Students then brainstorm, trying to uncover every word they can think of that is related to the stimulus word. As words are provided, they are grouped into an appropriate category. Discussion, of course, reveals the reasoning and the shades of meaning that define the categories.

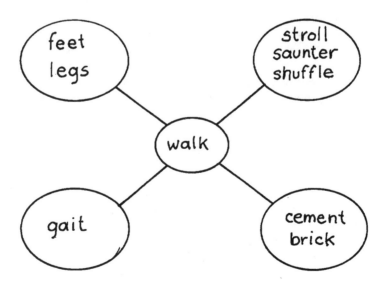

2.  *Team Games*—Divide the group in half and then call out a word from a book the class is reading. The first team must supply a synonym (or an antonym, or complete an analogy, or supply a word for a category—you may choose to

work on one or all of these). If successful, the team gets a point and the next team has a turn.

3. *Precise Language*—Try to demonstrate to students that the English language offers wonderful alternatives to overworked words. In fact, the use of more precise language helps readers visualize or comprehend more clearly. Encourage the use of a thesaurus and a dictionary.

   Have students act out a sentence such as "I like that book," *said* John, using replacements for *said*.

*EXAMPLES*  *stated, exclaimed, spoke, shouted, whispered, cried, asserted, uttered, expressed, voiced, affirmed, declared, proclaimed, articulated, mumbled, muttered, informed, announced, ranted.*

Choose a particularly vivid sentence from a book the class is reading and have students substitute common words for the expressive words to see how much less effective the sentence becomes.

*EXAMPLE*  How does the wind walk in autumn?

The wind walks in a rush,
brushing colored leaves
from the trees as she passes.
(*How Does the Wind Walk*, Carlstrom, 1993, p. 1)

might become "The wind blows fast, blowing colored leaves off the trees as it goes by."

4. *Practice*—Practice games and exercises that require students to think about a word in a variety of ways are useful. The words may be taken from the books that your students are reading. You may wish to create packs of words to accompany many of the books in your classroom. The following activities are examples of different kinds of practice:

   a. A deck of cards is used. A number of words with multiple meanings are selected (e.g., *box, point*). One word is written on each card. The first student picks a card and uses the word in a sentence. Each member of the group then thinks of a new sentence, using the word differently each time. This continues until a student cannot think of a sentence and therefore receives a point. A new word card is then chosen. The student with the least points at the end is the winner.

*EXAMPLES*  run

I can run fast.
I saw the water run off the counter.
My stocking has a run in it.
The movie had a long run.
He hit a home run.
There was a run on chicken soup at the market.
Is there a dog run in the back yard?

   b. A series of definitions can be written for a word, or dictionary definitions can be used. Sentences using the word in a variety of ways can be matched by students to the appropriate definition. This may also be used in card-game form (Concentration) where the appropriate definition is matchd to a sentence with an underlined word.

   c. An exercise with fifteen to twenty cloze sentences might have only three or four word choices for the deletions. Because each word would have to be used for several sentences, the sentences would require the use of each word in different ways.

5. *Puns Intended*—A young boy dressed in red pajamas was refusing to go to bed on time. "You're really making me see red," chuckled his mother.

     Punning is lots of fun. Use puns deliberately, corny as they may be. When kids discover that playing with language can be fun, they are more receptive to vocabulary building.

6. Writing activities help to reinforce understanding of vocabulary and concepts. When you have students respond to their reading in journals, you may wish to assign writing that utilizes the particular vocabulary from their books.

### Hear What We Have Here

Students frequently assign a word the meaning of its homophone. When discussing a word's meaning, it is often useful to introduce the homophone (if there is one) at the same time so that students may compare and contrast.

*EXAMPLE*

    He was asked to pay the *fare*.
    The test was *fair*.

### Rooting Out Meaning

By learning the meaning of prefixes, roots, and suffixes, the meanings of words are often revealed. Knowing that the prefix *dis-* means "the opposite of," the meanings of such words as *disappear, disprove,* and *dissatisfied* are easier to figure out. Students must watch out for words like *disk*, however, where *dis* is not a prefix.

    Introducing students to Latin and Greek roots will uncover still more words. The Latin word *porto* (carry) helps students understand many words particularly when common prefixes and suffixes are known.

*EXAMPLE*

    *transport*—to carry across
    *import*—to carry in
    *export*—to carry out
    *portable*—able to be carried

Dictionaries indicate whether a Greek or Latin root is present in a word. Students, when discovering a root, might attempt to find other words using the root. Have students participate in root searches. Or, assign one or two words at a time to see what students can compile to share with others in terms of roots, prefixes, suffixes, and related words.

### From Louis Pasteur—"Pasteurize"

Knowing how a word has entered the language offers students a larger framework within which to fit a new concept, and thereby increases the likelihood that the word will be remembered. Moreover, word histories often add interest and provide motivation for learning words. Appropriate source books are:

*Horsefeathers and Other Curious Words.* New York: Harper & Row, 1986.
*Thereby Hangs a Tale: Stories of Curious Word Origins.* New York: Harper & Row, 1985.
*Word Mysteries and Histories: From Quiche to Humble Pie* by the American Heritage Dictionary Editors. Boston: Houghton Mifflin, 1986.
*Guppies in Tuxedos: Funny Eponyms* by Marvin Terban. Clarion, 1988.
*Batty, Bloomers, and Boycott: A Little Etymology of Eponymous Words* by Rosie Boycott. New York: Peter Bedrick Books, 1983.

**A Word a Day**

Let each student select a word to be learned each day. Each student must use his or her word five times during the course of the day. Students should keep a booklet with a week's words on each page using sentences and/or pictures to illustrate the words. During a journal-writing exercise, frequently ask students to include the week's words in their story or literary creation.

**A Word a Week**

Ask students to find an unfamiliar word in their reading each Monday. It may be in any subject or from any book. Have them recount the subsequent number of times they encounter the word during the week, whether at home or school, orally, from television, or in reading. Chances are, students will be surprised at how often the word suddenly appears when previously it had never crossed their paths.

## SUGGESTIONS FOR IMPROVING THE USE OF CONTEXT

An understanding of different kinds of contextual clues helps students to notice unknown words and to note how the context has enabled them to achieve meaning. Certain contextual aids are simpler for students to recognize and use than others. Most students use contextual information when it appears in synonym form more easily than when it is present in inference form. You might be wise to use synonyms to demonstrate the use of contextual information to reveal an unknown word's meaning. Once students are able to use context in this way, the other kinds of cues should be taught. The most common categories include:

- *Definition or Synonym*—The definition or synonym of the unknown word appears in the makeup of the sentence itself (To *divulge* the news is to reveal it), in the following sentence (The news was *divulged* slowly. Bit by bit it was revealed), in apposition or parentheses, (The news was *divulged*, [revealed, slowly]), or in an example that follows (The news was *divulged* slowly, as one piece at a time was revealed.).
- *Antonym*—Frequently antonyms or word opposites are contrasted with the unknown word. The antonym, often a familiar word, may be signaled by the use of words such as: *but, however*, etc.

*EXAMPLE*    Jill was *reticent* but her sister was quite talkative.

- *Summary of Preceding Statements or Mood*—Many paragraphs develop an idea that is expressed by a single culminating word. Although the word may not be a part of students' receptive vocabulary, the preceding sentences cumulatively have revealed its meaning.

*EXAMPLES* **a.** Students were asked to sit a seat apart from each other. Everyone received three sheets of paper and two sharp pencils. No talking was allowed during the two hours of the *examination*.

**b.** The children dressed up for the event. Everyone came to help celebrate. It was a *festive* time.

- *Groupings of Words*—When related words appear successively, and readers are unfamiliar with one of the words, the grouping enables students to place the word in a category that helps to convey its meaning.

*EXAMPLE* Saws, hammers, and *awls* are essential to carpenters.

- *Similes*—Similes often reveal the meaning of an unknown term through comparison. The words *as* or *like* are used to communicate the comparison.

*EXAMPLES* Her skin was as white and transparent as *alabaster*.
Her white transparent skin was like *alabaster*.

- *Inference*—When the unfamiliar word is not defined in the text, the reader is frequently able to infer its meaning from the illustration(s) provided.

*EXAMPLE* Watching the huge meals she ate, I was not surprised by her *corpulence*.

**We Look But We Don't See**
Try to get students into the habit of underlining unfamiliar words in their reading even though the general meaning is understood from context. They should then go back to check on specific meaning. This provides an opportunity for students to check their contextual guesses against dictionary definitions. Underlining proves valuable because students pay attention to words and often find that they meet the same words again and again, words that they might previously have seen but not noted. This suggestion should be reserved for books at home that the students own.

**No Nonsense**
By substituting nonsense words in sentences, teachers can highlight the effectiveness of the context.

*EXAMPLE* The details of the news story were *pubosted* slowly. Each day brought new *pubostations*. What do *pubost* and *pubostations* mean?

**I've Got a Secret**
When asked to divulge how they have uncovered a word's meaning, students often articulate a strategy that they and others remember more easily than your explanation. Assistance in utilizing context appropriately can be given very naturally, for if one student has overlooked a relevant context clue, a peer may have the meaning key.

NAME: **Dominate**

SKILL: Meaning vocabulary—Synonyms

MATERIALS: Game board, markers

PROCEDURE:
1. Write two words on each domino. The examples may be used or vocabulary from any book the students are reading may be substituted.
2. There are twelve dominoes (1 to 12). Students start with the bottom half of 1 (scent) and look for its synonym on the top half of a domino, in this case at 9 (odor). They write the number 9 on the blank line that follows 1.
3. Now the player looks at the bottom half of 9 (expand), finds its synonym on the top half of another domino, and writes the number of that domino in the next blank.
4. The student continues until the top of 1 is reached.
5. It is helpful to put a check next to each domino that is used so that fewer dominoes will need to be searched each time.

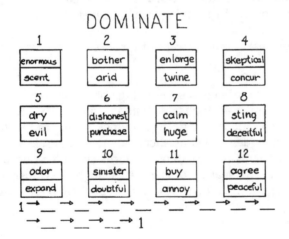

DOMINATE

| 1 | 2 | 3 | 4 |
|---|---|---|---|
| enormous | bother | enlarge | skeptical |
| scent | arid | twine | concur |

| 5 | 6 | 7 | 8 |
|---|---|---|---|
| dry | dishonest | calm | sting |
| evil | purchase | huge | deceitful |

| 9 | 10 | 11 | 12 |
|---|---|---|---|
| odor | sinister | buy | agree |
| expand | doubtful | annoy | peaceful |

1 → __ → __ → __ → __ → __ → __ → __ → __
→ __ → __ → __ → __ → 1

VARIATIONS: Vowels

| raw | Fred | sweep | dime |
|---|---|---|---|
| 1 ____ | 2 ____ | 3 ____ | 4 ____ |
| chap | trip | turn | brake |

| sill | lack | mute | perk |
|---|---|---|---|
| 5 ____ | 6 ____ | 7 ____ | 8 ____ |
| toast | trust | shock | haul |

| stay | grow | club | flop |
|---|---|---|---|
| 9 ____ | 10 ____ | 11 ____ | 12 ____ |
| dent | cube | find | treat |

1. Start with the bottom half of 1 (chap) and find a word with the same vowel sound on the top half of a domino.
2. Continue as described previously.

# DOMINATE

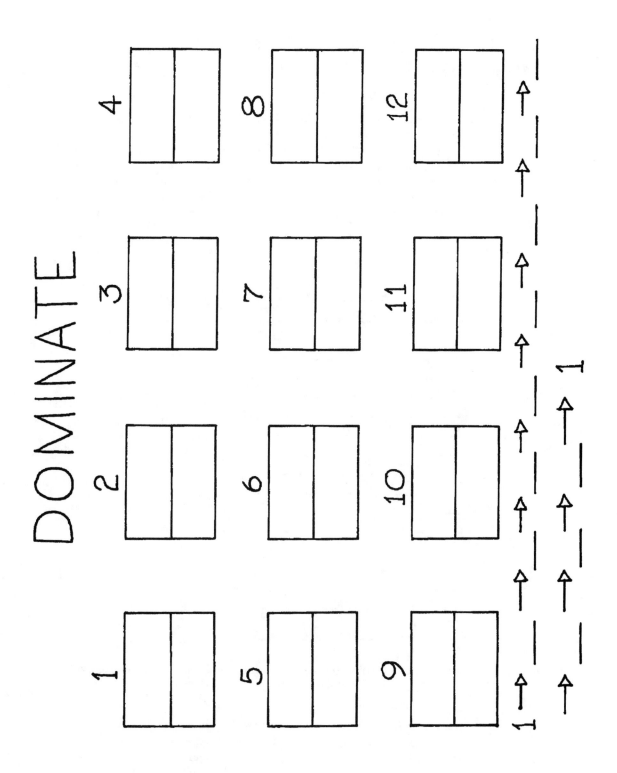

71

*NAME:* **The _____ Have It! (Yeas or Nays)*** 

*SKILL:* Multiple meanings and word connotations

*MATERIALS:* Game board, pencil, dictionary

*PROCEDURE:*
1. Ask students to read the words you have written on the top of the game board. Words from any book may be used.
2. Have them decide whether they feel positively (yea) or negatively (nay) about each word and write the word in the appropriate column.
3. Next to the word have the students defend their column choice.
4. When finished students add up the number of words in each column and fill in the blank in the title with Yea or Nay depending on which column has the most entries.

The ____ Have it !

1. Power  2. Dough  3. Slight  4. Odor  5. Plain

6. Squeal  7. Expand  8. Shallow  9. Ruffle  10. Relish

Yeas                         Nays

Total: _____ Total: _____

*VARIATION:* To practice distinguishing between fact and opinion: Mark sentences which are fact under *Yea* and those which are opinions under *Nay*.

| | |
|---|---|
| Tom has an odd accent. | The sun is shining. |
| Jane walks with a limp. | Carol seems distracted. |
| George is in for lunch. | Richard appears lost. |
| Sally is "out to lunch." | Michael has three appointments today. |
| It is a beautiful day. | Betsy has a busy day ahead. |

---

*Thanks to Isabel Beck and Margaret McKeown, "Learning Words Well: A Program to Enhance Vocabulary and Comprehension," *The Reading Teacher*, March 1983, pp. 622–625.

# The ___ Have it !

1. ___ 2. ___ 3. ___ 4. ___ 5. ___

6. ___ 7. ___ 8. ___ 9. ___ 10. ___

| Yeas | Nays |
|---|---|
| | |
| | |
| | |
| | |
| | |
| | |
| | |
| | |
| | |
| | |
| **Total:** | **Total:** |

# 7

# Literal Comprehension

True reading cannot take place without understanding. That is, pronouncing words without understanding them cannot be called reading. Most explanations of reading instruction treat word identification and comprehension separately merely to facilitate discussion. We have continued that tradition in this book.

Most discussions also distinguish literal from inferential comprehension, even though they are usually needed by the reader simultaneously. We separate these skills for convenience and because they can be taught separately first and then combined. Inferential comprehension will be discussed in Chapter 8.

Literal and inferential comprehension differ in one important respect. For literal comprehension to occur, readers need to understand what is actually on the page, while inferential understanding requires readers to go beyond the text to their own experiences.

It is important to note, however, that both kinds of comprehension require readers to bring their background and experiences to the text. Little, if any, understanding will take place if the vocabulary, syntax, and concepts are not familiar to readers. Therefore, "what's in readers' heads" is as important as what is in the text. Reading demands the integration of both categories, but literal understanding needs less of "what's in readers' heads" than does inferential.

As important as the distinction between literal and inferential is that between recognition and recall of literal information. Students may be able to locate data without being able to remember it, or vice versa. Because of this, memory for content and ability to locate it demand different teaching and assessment techniques.

Separating teaching from testing procedures for literal comprehension is another important consideration. The first, in the form of comprehension questions in oral or written form, is what often occurs in classrooms under the guise of comprehension instruction. Although questions can be teaching as well as testing tools, they must be selected or created with care, positioned at key points during the lesson, and used diagnostically to see which students need more help with which skill.

When literal comprehension takes place successfully, readers are able to identify the major components of a selection—the *who, what, when, where,* and *why* of sentences or larger text units. These are called the details of a selection. Students are also able to understand the order in which things happen in a story, often through the use of signal words like *first, afterwards,* and *finally.* Successful readers can also find or remember main ideas or themes when they are explicitly stated in titles, topics, or summarizing sentences. Anaphora, language devices such as pronouns and helping verbs that reduce repetition in speaking and writing, are understood by students who can comprehend literal meaning. So too are the meanings of individual words in a selection, but this chapter deals only with the comprehension of connected text. Word knowledge is discussed in Chapter 6.

## IDENTIFYING THE SKILL NEED

When students come to school without the background of experiences necessary to comprehend a particular selection, it is up to you to preteach the vocabulary and concepts that will enable them to understand what they will read.

If you teach beginning readers, you may find that in their zest to practice decoding, they overanalyze words, even those they can pronounce, and neglect comprehension. Here it's up to you to refocus students' attention on what they are reading about, as they deal with how to read it.

If you teach in the middle or upper grades, you've noticed that the stories and articles appropriate for those levels contain concepts and vocabulary that are often beyond the experiences and interests of your students. And selections at the middle and upper grades are longer, putting burdens on students' memories—they'll need to remember all parts of the story in order to understand the whole. At these levels, capturing students' interest, providing background for their reading, and helping them deal with longer units of text are essential literal comprehension techniques.

## TEACHING THE SKILL: TECHNIQUES AND ACTIVITIES

### SELECT READING MATERIAL CAREFULLY

Whenever possible, choose texts for your students that match their interests, reading ability, and the length of text with which they feel comfortable. Also, take care to choose well-written selections that highlight the textual characteristics you are interested in teaching. For instance, a lesson on literal main idea should involve material that has main ideas stated in topic sentences or titles, rather than inferred main ideas found in themes or morals.

When students must read a difficult text, it's a good idea to find another book on the same topic that's easier to read. The easier book may provide the background necessary to understand the harder text. Or you may want to modify or rewrite the difficult material for students, perhaps providing them with a clearly-written summary that they can read before or after you have read aloud the difficult text.

### WHAT'S THE POINT?

Main ideas of sentences can usually be located by identifying the subject and predicate. With longer units like paragraphs or chapters, sources for main ideas are: (1) topic or summarizing sentences, (2) boldface headings, and (3) subheadings, as well as (4) an author's clearly stated purposes for writing a particular piece. Students need to be shown examples of these and how to find them on their own. The following selections illustrate several ways that the literal main idea can be found in a paragraph.

**Use of Topic Sentence**
Columbus made a mistake when he called the people he met on San Salvador "Indians." He named them Indians because he believed that he had found the Indies. Instead, he had landed on the continent we call America. He should have called the people living there Americans!

**Use of Summarizing Sentence**
Columbus set sail from Spain for the Indies. He didn't realize that there was a continent in between Spain and the Indies. It was America, and Columbus landed on the island of San Salvador, which is part of Central America. Believing that he had landed in the Indies instead of in America, Columbus called the people he met there Indians instead of Americans.

**Use of Heading or Title**
Columbus Calls the Americans "Indians"
Columbus set sail from Spain to look for the Indies. He thought he had found it when he landed on San Salvador, on the American continent. So he called the people he found there Indians instead of Americans, and the name stuck.

RECOGNIZING DETAILS

To help students find details as they read:

1. Show them how to turn a question into a partial statement and then scan for the answer. For example, if a selection deals with a wrasse, a fish that changes gender during the course of its maturation, change the question *How long does*

   *it take a female to become a male?* to the cloze statement: It *takes* _____

   _____ *for the female to become a male,* and have students scan the selection for key words having to do with quantity (*many, few, seven*) and time (*hour, days, months*).
2. At the beginning stages of helping students to recognize details, give them the location of answers to detail questions. Tell them the page, paragraph, sentence, or line from which information can be obtained. (e.g., p. 56, ¶2, line 8). Over the course of several lessons, gradually withdraw the amount of information until only the page number remains.
3. Because much information is often presented in sentences, it becomes important to be able to reduce that information to essential noun–predicate statements and also to be able to isolate kernel ideas from embellished or embedded ones. This latter skill is illustrated below. Students may need to break down sentences into many kernels at first, but they will need fewer kernel sentences later.
   a. Embedded sentence: Ellen's story about a tall, dark man with pointy teeth, whose mind was crawling with snakes and demons, made my hair stand on end.

Kernel sentences:
Ellen told a story.
It was about a man.
He was tall and dark.
He had pointy teeth.
His mind was crawling with snakes and demons.
The story made my hair stand on end.

**b.** Embedded sentence: Despite his friend's warning, Will backed into the wet paint, ruining his new suit.

Kernel sentences:
Will's friend warned him.
The warning was about wet paint.
Will backed into the paint anyway.
His new suit was ruined.

**c.** Embedded sentence: Mr. Larkin, the captain of the men's volleyball team, believes it's not how you play the game, but whether you win or lose that counts.

Kernel sentences:
Mr. Larkin is the captain of the mens' volleyball team.
He doesn't care much about how you play the game.
But he does care whether you win or lose.

**4.** Teaching the five W's helps students locate the who, what, when, where, and why of a sentence, paragraph, or story. A chart format such as the one presented below can be particularly useful. Of course, not every sentence will contain all of these demands.

| Who | What | When | Where | Why |
|---|---|---|---|---|
| Marcia | bought a magazine | Saturday | at the drugstore | because it had pictures of her favorite rock group |
| Bo | missed the trolley, but he wasn't upset | | In Tunaville | |
| Aunt Rea | telephoned and invited us for dinner | on Sunday | at her house | when she won a turkey in a raffle |
| The horse outside | made its move, catching the favorite | suddenly | at the wire | |

## REMEMBERING DETAILS

To help students retain details from their reading:

**1.** Tell them what to look for in advance. This is often called asking purpose questions. Be selective about what you ask. No more than three items should be requested, and, if possible, the details should be related—all names of characters or all traits of a character, for example. Small numbers of facts and their interrelatedness maximize the opportunity for success with this task.

2. Teach note-taking skills. Somtimes just the act of placing a tiny pencil mark beside the information to be remembered will help to recall it later. Allowing students to jot down the answers to purpose questions when they come upon them in their reading and to refer to their notes during assessment instead of going back to the text helps bridge the gap between locating and remembering information.

3. Begin instruction with smaller chunks of text (phrase, sentence) to limit the number of details. Gradually increase the amount of text and number of details to be processed.

4. Help students retell narratives by providing cues such as illustrations or key words from the story. Instead of discarding old basal texts or storybooks, separate the text and illustrations. Have students read or listen to the story and then retell it using the pictures as a guide. Gradually, fewer illustrations and key words will be needed to prompt students' narratives.

5. Encourage students to create mental images of settings and characters, when such information is available. This can be done with the aid of illustrations at first, and later without them.

## GIVE HELP IN DISTINGUISHING MAIN IDEAS FROM DETAILS

Two kinds of diagrams help students conceptualize the difference between a main idea and its details. One visual display is a box with a kind of cover or lid, with the main idea in the lid and the supporting details in the box. This works for paragraphs in which the main idea is found in the topic sentence, as shown. When the main idea is found in the concluding sentence, invert the diagram to put the lid on bottom, making a brimmed hat!

> The functions of the hemispheres of the brain are quite different.
> One hemisphere is verbal, analytic.
> The other is artistic, intuitive and mute.
> This nonspeaking side is usually on the right.
> It is currently the focus of much research.
> The two brain sides are linked by nerves.
> Damaged nerves? The sides can't communicate!

Another visual display is called a semantic web, with the main idea at the center and the supporting details radiating out as strands. This web illustrates an episode from the book *Delilah* by Carole Hart.

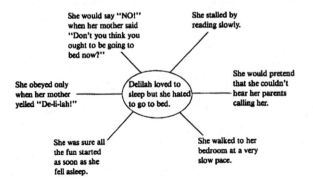

## ORDER COUNTS

Sequencing is important for establishing (1) the logical order of events in a story, (2) the chronological events in historical text, (3) the steps of a recipe, and (4) construction directions. Suggestions for help with sequence are:

- Teach the meaning and use of signal words such as: *first, second, next, after, before, then, finally, following,* even earlier. The words are excellent prompts to encourage a story retelling.
- Teach cause–effect relationships as another kind of sequence. Here, details or events do not simply follow or accompany each other, but one event or detail clearly precipitates the other. Signal words and phrases such as *if/then, why/because, happened before, caused by, the effect of,* help to cue comprehension of cause/effect sequences.
- Provide visual displays such as outlines, timelines, or flow charts to help conceptualize the events in a sequence. Time-honored techniques also include the use of cut-up comic strips or paragraphs from a story, which students put in order using logic or signal words.

## IMPROVING YOUR QUESTIONS

Too many of the literal questions asked during comprehension assess knowledge of unimportant details. To expand the usefulness of questions as instruction aids, they should be few in number, carefully crafted, given before the selection, and then used diagnostically during a lesson.

In addition, the way you respond to student answers can redirect and expand comprehension. For questions to be truly instructional, discussions should follow student answers, whether those answers are accurate or not. Requiring students to show where they found their answers and to give more than a "yes" or "no" may take time, but better comprehension will result.

It is important to realize that even with literal questions, which seemingly have only one right answer, a divergent response may also be correct. For example, you might ask a student "Why did Goldilocks enter the bears' home?" after it was stated in the story that she went in because no one was home. If the student answers "Because she was nosy," you need to realize that the student may be answering the question based on her/his own experiences. Perhaps in that student's family, courage and curiosity are labeled "nosiness." Under these and similar circumstances, ask students for reasons for their answers. Divergent answers should be rewarded whenever possible. This discussion should reveal that the line between literal and inferential comprehension can't always be sharply drawn.

## WHAT AM I LOOKING FOR?

It's a good idea to help students "psych" questions—that is, decide what kind of answering mode questions ask for. Should students look back in the story for an answer or try to think it out on their own? Often the language of the question will help students make that decision.

Show students that with literal questions, they can scan the selection for key words from the question. When they find them, they will probably be in the vicinity of the answer. Sometimes key words can be found in two different parts of the text. Then students need to integrate the information from those parts to arrive at the answer. Usually, when a question asks students what they think, believe, or feel about something, the question is calling for inferencing.

## LET ME ASK YOU

Guide students to ask questions of their texts. This may help them to improve their memory for content, become more independent readers, and develop good study habits. You might want to model this process for them, using a selection with boldface headings that can become questions. Or have students "walk through" a selection and look at the pictures. Ask them to raise questions about the pictures and then read the accompanying text to find answers.

## DISTINGUISH BETWEEN LITERAL AND FIGURATIVE MEANINGS

Students need to be able to separate literal from figurative expressions. It's adorable to see a toddler dip his eye into a glass of milk at his mother's warning to "keep your eye on the milk!" But readers need to differentiate between phrases such as "Wait sixty seconds," and "Wait a minute." (The former connotes "Time it, please," while the latter says "Don't actually watch the clock as you wait for me, but I shouldn't be very long.") The best activities to develop this skill have students matching literal and figurative equivalent expressions, and then eventually providing literal expressions for figurative ones.

| *Figurative* | *Literal* |
|---|---|
| Joey hit the road. | Joey left in his car. |
| Paco is a clam. | Paco keeps his mouth shut. |
| Read between the lines. | Infer the author's message. |

## PARAPHRASING

1.  Underline certain words in passages and have students generate synonymous terms (similar, but not identical in meaning) for them.
    Francine is a <u>nice</u> girl.
    *pleasant* or *well-mannered*
    Will you <u>have</u> another piece?
    *take* or *eat*
2.  Have students rewrite sentences, inverting the word order.
    Louise and Shirley were playing softball,
    when there was a strange noise from space.

    A strange noise from space occurred when
    Louise and Shirley were playing softball.
3.  Let students make up questions for a selection. Tell them good (harder-to-answer) questions are those that use different, but synonymous words from those used in the text. Challenge them to make up "killer questions" for you.
4.  Do a sentence-by-sentence reading of a selection. After each sentence is read, have students tell about it in their own words. Copy the student-generated sentences and compare these to the original text for synonymous terms.

## SHE, HE, IT

Sometimes authors use substitute terms, pronouns, and auxiliary verbs called anaphora, to reduce redundancy in a text and provide variety. Unless readers can identify the referent for an anaphora, they may have difficulty understanding a sentence and, in some cases, an entire selection.

Practice sentences that require identification of anaphora are recommended. Provide matching sentences, one with anaphora and the other without, so students can see how "silly" the second sentence sounds.

I enjoyed that movie more than Tyrone did.
I enjoyed that movie more than Tyrone enjoyed that movie.

My sheets feel awfully cold when I crawl into them.
My sheets feel awfully cold when I crawl into my sheets.

Franklin and Suzanne ate dinner after they watched MTV.
Franklin and Suzanne ate dinner after Franklin and Suzanne watched MTV.

NAME: **Unlock the Meaning**

SKILL: Matching synonymous expressions

MATERIALS: Game board, a set of 12 cut-out keys

PROCEDURE:
1. Use the key template to make 12 cutout shapes.
2. Twelve sentences that contain synonymous expressions (six matches) are printed one each on the keys, which are then placed face down over the key outlines on the game board.
3. Students turn over two keys at a time.
4. If a match is made, the keys are kept and a point is won. If students can also identify key phrases within the sentences that match or are roughly equivalent, they may gain an additional point for each.
5. For example, there are four potential phrase matches in the sentences:
   a. Sue and Brian help out at the bakery after school.
   b. They work as baker's assistants from 5 to 6 on weekdays.
   - They are: Sue and Brian/They
   - help out/work
   - from 4 to 6 on weekdays/after school
   - at the bakery/baker's assistants

   If students find all four, their total point count for that turn would be 5, 1 for the sentence match, and 4 for phrase matches.
6. If no match is found, the keys are turned face down again for another turn.

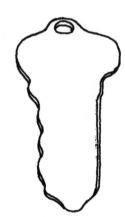

*Sentence pairs for keys:*

I hope you can come to my party.
Mindy, will you join us at my house Saturday night?

That dress is too small on you.
Annie, look how tight that outfit is!

The soccer game ended with a loss for our team
We didn't win the kicking contest.

Let's spread the picnic out here.
We can put the food on that table.

A magical creature came out of the woods.
An enchanting elf appeared through an opening in the thicket.

Are you feeling sad?
Why are you so glum, chum?

VARIATIONS: Synonyms *(moist/damp)*, antonyms *(moist/dry)*, or figurative-literal *(I could eat a horse)/(I'm very hungry)* matches could be printed on the keys.

# UNLOCK THE MEANING

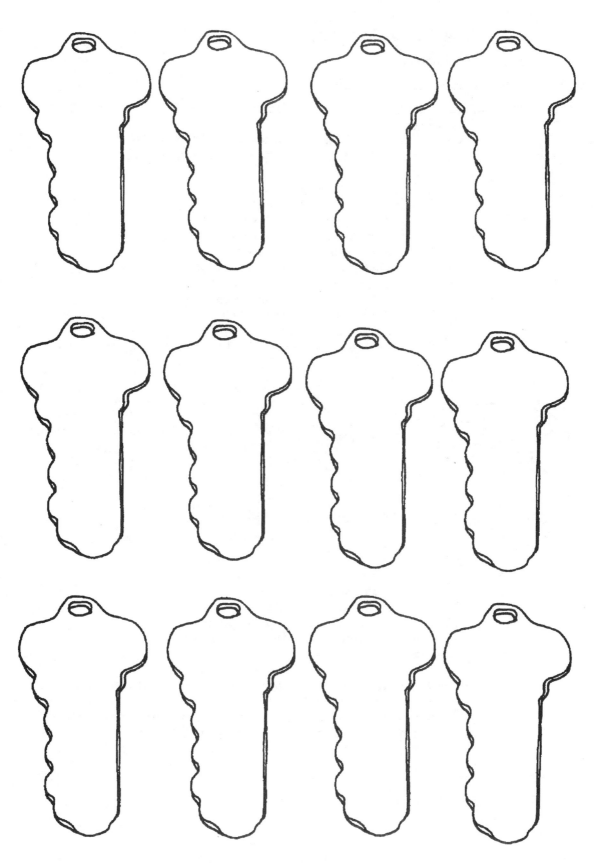

83

NAME: **Little Things Mean a Lot**

SKILL: Detail comprehension

MATERIALS: Game board, colored markers

PROCEDURE:
1. Add details to the game board drawings to grossly or subtly distinguish one drawing from the others.
2. Use the following directions or make up your own set. You may want to give oral or written directions, depending on what your students need.

| | |
|---|---|
| Couch: | Circle the messy couch. |
| | Draw a line under the neat couch. |
| Girls: | Put an X under the girl with the handbag. |
| | Draw a circle around the girl with the shoulder bag. |
| | Star the girl with the paper bag. |
| House: | Circle the house with no chimney. |
| | Underline the house with two chimneys. |
| | Color in the house with one chimney. |
| Shelf: | Print "bookshelf" on the shelf with only books on it. |
| | Put a star on the shelf with several tall books on it. |
| | Cross out the shelf with books and other things on it. |

  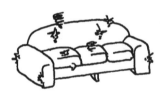

VARIATIONS:
- Try these distinguishing details on the game board:

| | |
|---|---|
| Couch: | many pillow, no pillows, one pillow |
| | striped, dotted, plaid |
| Girl: | mad, glad, sad |
| | skirt and blouse, pajamas, slacks, and sweater |
| House: | flowers, shrubs, vegetable garden |
| | on windows: blinds, curtains, shades |
| Shelves: | Anything goes! |

- This activity can be done by students, who can take turns adding details to the pictures, creating the directions, and responding.
- To provide practice with instructional vocabulary, you can simplify the differences among pictures, and give the directions orally.

# LITTLE THINGS MEAN A LOT

85

# 8

# Inferential Comprehension

Comprehension, as we have stated in Chapter 7, is often described as a literal process when readers depend heavily on the information in the text and as an inferential process when there is a greater use of the readers' prior knowledge. Commonly, inferential comprehension is defined as the ability to read between the lines. More specifically, it occurs as readers make predictions or develop ideas; when, for example, main idea, sequence, character, mood, and/or outcomes are not directly stated in the text.

Making inferences happens naturally in our daily lives. If we spy a young man, who is attempting to open a locked car door search his pockets, we easily recognize that he is looking for his key. So it is with written material, as well. "The sky darkened, though it was midafternoon, and suddenly the clouds let loose. Jane ran back to the house to get her _____ ." If a student is able to decode the words in the above passage, it is likely that appropriate choices for the missing word such as *raincoat, umbrella,* and *rainhat* will quickly come to mind. Yet, nowhere was it stated directly that it was raining.

The inferential process occurs at two levels. Conclusions drawn from reading sometimes occur when two or more ideas are directly stated in the text but the relationship is inferred by the readers. In H. A. Rey's *Curious George Gets a Medal* (1957), the text reads "George did not know what a museum was. He was curious. While the guard was busy reading his paper, George slipped inside" (page 30). Students may conclude that George went into the museum because he was curious about what a museum holds. The connection between George's curiosity and his entering the museum is certainly implied in the writing, although it is not stated directly.

At other times, readers must refer to their own prior knowledge or mental script to reach a conclusion. Adventurous students might determine that George went into the museum because it presented a challenge. After seeing the guard outside reading the paper, George was curious to see if he could enter without the guard noticing him. Students reaching this conclusion are injecting what might be their own personal reaction to the given circumstances.

In all instances, the ability to comprehend material at an inferential level is highly dependent upon how much readers bring to the text in background knowledge of both vocabulary and experiences. In order to make inferences about a given text, readers must have some mental concepts stored that help them to see relationships between ideas in the text. It is the ability to relate the written material to this personal background knowledge that permits inferential comprehension to occur.

If students eat mushrooms regularly at home, but have never heard that there are poisonous varieties that grow wild, they will not comprehend the reference in a story that says, "After eating the mushrooms she'd picked in the woods, Maria soon was in real trouble." Perhaps the only schema students can relate this sentence to is one about the legality or illegality of picking plants that are not on your own property. It is trouble with the law that these students will expect, rather than illness. Inferencing has occurred, students have translated the word *trouble* into what appears to be a plausible explanation, but the inference is wrong because they lacked appropriate background.

Related skills influence inferencing ability. Students who recognize and understand implied connectives, connotative meaning, and figurative language, who have a sense of story structure, and who have a mind-set for ambiguity are apt to be the most successful at discerning the inferences in an author's message.

## IDENTIFYING THE SKILL NEED

Class discussions or readers' responses in their literature journals may reveal some difficulties with making inferences. These responses may reveal either a lack of student preparedness or a lack of textual clarity. As indicated previously, all students benefit from an emphasis on greater background knowledge or breadth of meaning vocabulary. When students do not have the language experiences that allow for understanding multiple meanings, figurative language, and other connotative aspects of words, they may miss the allusion, intentional pun, or implied humor or irony in a passage.

*EXAMPLES*      That's a *cool* dress.
She was on *pins and needles* waiting for the mail to arrive.

Sometimes students need to be reminded that authors expect readers to use their background experiences as they read. If readers interact with the text in this way, they are able to draw conclusions about the textual material without the authors having to spell out every thought.

You may find that you have to help students recognize character traits, cause and effect relationships, and sequential relationships when they are implied. Figurative language, especially metaphors, and literary techniques like irony can be troublesome. Students may also need to be alerted that text can be ambiguous or subject to differing interpretations. "Because Peter finished his homework, he was able to read that book" may be interpreted as a cause-and-effect sequential relationship: Once his homework was done, Peter had time to read that book for pleasure; or as a simple cause-and-effect relationship: What Peter learned by doing his homework enabled him to read that book for pleasure. Often, although not always, the remainder of the paragraph will clarify which meaning was intended, but students may be confused by ambiguity and lose their concentration for the remaining writing.

## TEACHING THE SKILL: TECHNIQUES AND ACTIVITIES

### WHAT DO YOU KNOW

Be sure to help students review what they know about the subject matter before reading a selection. By looking at the title and the first sentence or paragraph, show them that what they already know helps them to anticipate what the selection might reveal. It is important for students to recognize that comprehending involves relating information on the page to prior understanding. Comprehension demands active readers who respond to material by accepting or rejecting the information on the page, and in the process, expand or confirm their prior knowledge.

Sometimes a useful technique is to have students list everything they know about the topic in one column. In a second column, have them list what they want or hope to learn in the text, and in a third column, have them list what they did learn after reading the text. This exercise provides a graphic means of uncovering misconceptions, helps students relate the new material to their prior knowledge, helps organize the new material, and often motivates future reading.

### DIRECT TEACHING

1. Show students directly with examples that much of what they understand after reading a sentence (paragraph, selection) has not been stated openly by the author. For example, in Rosemary Wells' *Moss Pillows—A Voyage to the Bunny Planet* (1992), the first sentence reads:

    "Robert had to ride in the backseat of the car for four hours of turnpike driving."

    Do you think Robert enjoyed the ride?

    Do you think Robert expected that something exciting was going to happen?

    Did Robert expect this to be a good day or a bad day? Do you think he was in a good mood?

    Help students to see that, by putting themselves in Robert's shoes and thinking about how it feels to ride for a long time in the backseat of a car, they can understand a lot more about Robert than the author has actually told them.

2. Continue by having students supply reasonable inferences for the next page.

    "He and his family arrived at Uncle Ed and Aunt Margo's at 3:30 in the afternoon on the first Sunday in February."

    Examples of reasonable inferences:

    Robert was happy that the ride was over.

    Robert was happy to see his aunt and uncle.

    Robert was expecting to have fun now that they had arrived.

    Demonstrate how sometimes tentative inferences are made and then discarded as more information is added. The new facts must be noted and students must be flexible enough to revise their thinking as they read. The next three pages read:

    "Ed and Margo's four boys all piled on top of him at once. Just before dinner Ed and Margo were bitten by the argument bug. Dinner was cold liver chili. All evening Robert had to hide from the boys."

## CHARACTER TRAITS

Help students to recognize that much of what we learn about people and events in reading is not stated directly but rather is suggested by the examples given. This requires that students infer the "missing" adjectives. Give students examples from their reading like the following:

In Erickson's *A Toad for Tuesday* (1974), when Wharton risks his life to bring beetle brittle to his aunt because he thought she'd enjoy some, we can think of him as thoughtful, without the author having to use this word specifically to describe him. Moreover, if we read elsewhere that Tom was generous and friendly but his brother was just the opposite, we do not have to see the word *stingy* to apply it to Tom's brother.

## CLASSIFYING QUESTIONS

Have students attempt to ask questions about selections they read. Using the text, have them divide their questions into those which can be answered directly by the words in the text and those which require using their prior knowledge. Writing questions and having to recognize the kind of thinking called for will help students to utilize these thinking skills while reading.

*EXAMPLE*    In Russell Erickson's *A Toad for Tuesday*, one sentence reads, "After he had gone quite a way and when the sun was directly overhead he decided to have some lunch" (page 15). A literal question would ask where the sun was when Wharton decided to have lunch. An inferential question requiring prior knowledge would ask "What time was it when Wharton decided to have lunch?"

## CORRECTING STRATEGIES

Help students to be aware of whether they have comprehended while reading. If students recognize that something is wrong, they can attempt different strategies to clarify misunderstandings or a lack of comprehension.

1. Reread the problem area and try to make sense of it.
2. Reread the material that preceded the troublesome sentence or paragraph to note details they may have missed.
3. Continue reading to see if what comes next explains the confusing part.
4. Look for specific vocabulary that may be causing or contributing to the confusion. Students may need to look up words for unfamiliar meanings.

During each of these steps, because inferencing does not always occur without some instruction, students should be watching for: (1) unstated connectives (cause-effect, comparison, conditional, sequential—see "Identifying the Skill Need"), and (2) ways to relate the material to what they already know about the subject.

## FIGURATIVE LANGUAGE

Help students to recognize comparisons made through similes, metaphors, and personification. Show how each of these devices is used for emphasis.

*EXAMPLE*   His remark was very embarrassing.

     **a.**   Her cheeks turned as red as her ruby ring.
     **b.**   Her cheeks turned into fiery rubies.

Both the simile and the metaphor above compare the color of her blushing cheeks to rubies, deep red stones. By providing the students with a mental picture, these figures of speech emphasize the point.

Have students write similes using *like* and *as* and then write the comparisons as metaphors. The familiarity that writing brings will transfer awareness to reading.

Use the same rationale for teaching personification.

*EXAMPLE*   In *How Does The Wind Walk* (Carlstrom, 1993), one page reads: "The wind walks in a whirl, twirling the leaves around and around, before she waltzes them down streets and scatters them in faraway places." Does the wind walk? Can the wind waltz? Why does the author treat the wind as a person? Help students to see that the mental picture the sentence creates emphasizes the point in a way that is more effective than saying, "The wind blew the leaves around and around, before blowing them down streets to faraway places."

## HUMOR

Use cartoons and comics to emphasize double entendres. Show that it is the use of double meanings that makes them humorous. The newspaper is an excellent source for material.

Riddles and puns also use double meanings to achieve humor. use these with students, having them make up riddles or puns themselves so that they become accustomed to this use.

*EXAMPLE*   What has an eye but can't see? A needle or a potato.

## KNOW THE FACTS

In order to interpret or react to information, students must note and recall what has actually been stated. Ask students to find the facts that allow them to make inferences. For example, in the sentence given earlier, "Robert had to ride in the backseat for four hours of turnpike driving," is there enough information given for students to know whether Robert was excited or unhappy about the car ride? Since it only becomes clear as the story progresses, students need to learn to make tentative predictions until they have enough confirming data.

## WHAT HAPPENS NEXT?

Ask students to read part of a story and to predict what might occur next. Help students to identify the information already given that they must use to make predictions. By integrating what appears on the page with the students' prior knowledge or understandings about what has happened, a number of reasonable scenarios can be devised. These can be compared to the actual continuation of the story.

For example, in H. A. Rey's *Curious George Gets a Medal*, George lifts the gate latch to catch the large pig standing near the gate. Students can anticipate the trouble George will have because everything he has attempted to that point has backfired, leaving him more deeply involved.

An alternative activity might be to remove the last frame of a comic strip from the newspaper and ask students to try to write an appropriate frame. This can be compared to the frame that has been removed. Students often improve upon the humor.

Understanding story structure helps students with predictions, because they can anticipate what should occur next. See Chapter 10 for an explanation of story grammar.

## IT'S ALL RIGHT TO DISAGREE

Stress to students that the opinions they form about character, mood, or events are suggested by what has been stated in the text. The text, however, is open to differing interpretations by individual students. Using the example above from Erickson's *A Toad for Tuesday*, one student may find Wharton brave and thoughtful to want to risk danger in bringing his aunt some beetle brittle, while another may find him foolish, selfish, and insensitive to risk his life and desert his brother over such a minor deed. Even if the author tends to lead the student to react kindly toward Wharton and reinforces this by later selfless acts of Wharton's, it is not unreasonable to react differently if what is stated can substantiate that contradictory point of view as well.

## SIGNAL WORDS AND CONNECTIVES

Teach students what connectives to expect in prose and give them examples of sentences in which connectives have been omitted. Let students see the relationships themselves.

*EXAMPLE*    *Sequence:* "Jane walked to the store and then went for lunch, not coming home until 3:00" might read, "Jane walked to the store. She went for lunch. She did not come home until 3:00." It is not clear in the second version that Jane went for lunch after going to the store. It could as easily be read that Jane went to the store for lunch.

## MAIN IDEA

Understanding the main idea when it is not stated directly involves recognizing how what has been stated relates to a category.

1.  Playing categories with students by asking them to supply the categories for the examples you give (for example: *velvet, wool, silk, cotton = fabric*) helps to clarify what you are looking for.
2.  Recognizing a sentence that does not belong in a paragraph aids students in seeing that paragraphs or selections are developed around a particular idea.

*EXAMPLE*    Jane and Jill like to play jacks together. Playing board games was another interest they shared. Jane's grandmother lived with her family. Jane and Jill even enjoyed reading to each other.

3. Finally, matching (from a choice of three titles, choosing one for a paragraph) and then supplying a title ("Sharing the Fun" might be appropriate for the example given) shows students how to relate ideas.

## MODELING

Showing students how you think when you read is one of the most effective instructional tools you have. Using some examples from earlier in this chapter, model appropriate ways of reacting to reading by reading a sentence aloud and then saying "Oh, this tells me that Tom's brother is stingy," or "If the sun was overhead, that means it's noon," or "I think the author is trying to show that Jane and Jill are good friends," or "Oh yes, I thought that Wharton was kind and caring when he wanted to bring beetle brittle to his aunt, and now I see that I was right because he's saving the owl's life."

# Activities to Go

NAME: **Jumping to Conclusions**

SKILL: Making inferences

MATERIALS: Game board, sentence cards

PROCEDURE: 
1. The student begins at box 1 and picks a sentence card (examples follow). At least two inferences can be made for each sentence.*
2. If the students can make at least one inference, they move to the next box and pick a new card. Multiple inferences, however, should be encouraged.
3. Play continues until box 8 is completed.

*Sentences for cards:*

1. Cindy was all dressed up, wearing a red skirt and sweater, and red bows on the new shoes her mom had just bought her.
2. Jed watched the screen, sitting glued to his seat for the whole two hours.
3. Zachary jumped on the brakes of his car and stopped just in time.
4. First Chip got out a map of the city, and then he and Connie pulled over to the side of the road to plan their day.
5. Dan had to go to school that day, so he carried a box of tissues with him.
6. Emily happily sat in her seat and looked down to the center ring where the lions were doing tricks.
7. David asked for seconds of eggs and juice before he gathered his books and left.
8. The snow looked clean and white but Michael knew it meant a lot of trouble for him.
9. Beth put on her boots and raincoat and carried her umbrella in her briefcase as she left for work.
10. Lee nervously packed his suitcase with his clothes for the next seven days as he prepared for the flight that would take him to see his father and stepmother.
11. The ten-inning game ended as Ann ran around the bases and crossed home plate.
12. Geoff called to say he'd be home in an hour and that the family should eat now and not wait for him.
13. Jon ran to pet the dog, who quickly climbed into his lap.
14. Jenna was glad she'd worn boots because the path to the barn was muddy.
15. Wait until I change into a suit and then I'll race you to the raft.
16. When he got up during the night to go to the bathroom, Gordon tripped over a toy he'd left out.

VARIATION: Pick a card with a figurative expression and explain what is really meant. Examples: It was raining cats and dogs. Has the cat got your tongue? There's no use crying over spilled milk. He was seeing red. John was in the doghouse.

---

*If the first card reads, "Sarah gobbled down her food, the carrots included," the inferences could be:
  She had not eaten all day.
  She finished eating quickly.
  She did not have a stomach flu.
  She does not usually eat carrots.

# JUMPING TO CONCLUSIONS

NAME: **Tic Tacky Toe**

SKILL: Cause and effect

MATERIALS: Game board, two pens (two different color inks)

PROCEDURE:
1. Students play regular Tic Tac Toe using C (Cause) and E (effect) instead of X and O.
2. The first student chooses a block, reads the top sentence, and then puts a C next to whichever sentence below describes the cause of the action in the top sentence.
   There was a gas crisis.
   a. Cars were lined up at the gas stations.   __
   b. The Arab countries would not sell oil to the U.S.   _C_
   The student who is using E would have chosen sentence *a*.
3. The first student to have three correct C's or E's in a vertical, horizontal, or diagonal row wins. Sometimes the less obvious answer will be correct if students can justify their responses.

| He painted his house. | Tom ate a big meal. | The dog barked loudly. |
|---|---|---|
| a. The paint on the house was peeling.   __ | a. Tom felt filled.   __ | a. Sally held her dog tightly.   __ |
| b. The house looked fresh and clean.   _E_ | b. Tom was hungry.   __ | b. The mailman came up the walk.   __ |
| The bell rang. | Her toe was hurting. | The leaves were falling. |
| a. The students left the class.   __ | a. She looked at her foot.   _E_ | a. It was late September.   __ |
| b. The boy walked up to the house.   __ | b. There was a pebble in her shoe.   __ | b. The sidewalks were slippery in the rain.   __ |
| Jane was learning to read. | The baby was crying. | Peter missed a day of school. |
| a. Jane was in first grade.   __ | a. The mother picked up the baby.   __ | a. Peter had a lot of schoolwork to do.   _E_ |
| b. Jane could read to her family.   __ | b. The baby was hungry.   __ | b. Peter was sick.   __ |

*VARIATIONS:*   Vowel Digraphs, blends:

1. Each student uses a vowel digraph in place of X and O.
2. Each student uses a different color ink.

|  | r __l | m __l | b__t |
|---|---|---|---|
| X = ea | l__d | f __r | l__n |
| O = ai | h__l | m__n | r__d |

Synonyms or antonyms:

1. Students in turn fill in a synonym or antonym for the word they have chosen (X = synonym, O = antonym).
2. Each student uses a different color ink.

| ancient | morose | terse |
|---|---|---|
| lethal | amiable | potent |
| erect | blatant | adamant |

# Tic Tacky Toe

X = ""  O = ""

# 9

# Critical Comprehension

## DESCRIBING THE SKILL

A statement appearing in print may be true, blatantly false, or perhaps a distorted version of the truth. The fact that material is published is no guarantee of its validity. And yet often people defend a belief by claiming, "I read it in a book."

Critical reading is an essential part of comprehending. It occurs as readers evaluate what is read in the context of their experiences and/or external standards. As readers meet new information, they accept or reject its validity. To do this, they must integrate the new information into their existing cognitive structures, rejecting the new material when it conflicts with existing knowledge that has not been shown to be accurate.

Students consequently need adequate background knowledge about the material they are reading. If they have no cognitive structure against which to verify or negate new material, it is usually accepted at face value. Students reading that mononucleosis is a bacterial disease would have no way of reacting to this statement other than to accept it, if they (a) had never heard of mononucleosis or (b) did not know what was meant by bacterial disease.

Critical reading requires that a judgment be made. Readers may evaluate the relevance of the material, the accuracy of fact, and the reliability of the source. They may also be concerned with the validity of the conclusions and whether all needed facts are present. To make these judgments, readers take into account: author intent, point of view, background, and use of language. Often the judgments concern such topics as reality or fantasy, fact or opinion, bias, and propaganda. Whereas literal comprehension deals primarily with facts, and inferential comprehension with interpretation, critical comprehension is concerned with opinion, albeit substantiated opinion, and necessitates the use of both literal and inferential comprehension skills.

Clearly, critical reading demands analytical skills. Students must challenge the text with questions such as "Why?" or "Why not?" or "Do I agree?" or "So what?" To read critically means that readers must be skeptics. Students must be able to suspend judgment until the reading is completed and all of the material has been considered.

## IDENTIFYING THE SKILL NEED

As students discuss or write about literature and content material, you should be able to see the extent to which they use critical reading skills. It is important to directly teach critical reading skills. Particularly in the upper grades, as texts become more abstract, with more complex vocabulary and sentence structure, we cannot rely on students to intuit these skills.

You may want to review the kinds of questions that students should ask themselves as they read. For example, as students are reading *Little House on the Prairie* (Laura Ingalls Wilder, 1953), they might be wondering, "Is this a true story and if not, could this have happened?" "Has the author given an accurate picture of the times and circumstances?" It is important to make sure that students have adequate background knowledge, and to help students know where to go to find material to verify what they are reading. In other instances, for example, when students read about cold-blooded dinosaurs or an account of the Civil War, checking copyright dates and knowing something about an author's background may reveal obsolete information or bias.

You may also be looking to see if students (a) show an awareness that authors have purposes for writing, and (b) are making judgments as to whether these purposes have been met satisfactorily. Student recognition that propaganda techniques are present is another skill that you may look for.

## TEACHING THE SKILL: TECHNIQUES AND ACTIVITIES

### HE WHO HESITATES IS LOST

We teach critical reading skills right from the start when we ask young children "Could this really have happened? Why or why not?" "Did you like_____?" (the main character in the story) "Did you like what she did?" "Was this a good ending to the story?" Relating stories to personal experience and standards should continue when students begin to read for themselves, but because students at first are caught up with decoding and simple comprehension concerns, the habit of reacting critically can be lost. Teachers should not hesitate to teach critical reading skills at all levels of ability or to ask evaluative questions even with simple stories.

### VALID OR NOT?

Help students to be aware of features that question the authenticity or validity of a piece of writing—anachronisms, gross exaggerations, illogical or questionable conclusions. Certain cue words signal that a conclusion has been reached: *therefore, and so, from this we can see, in conclusion,* etc. Students should question whether the statement that follows has been adequately explained or prepared for. In his book *Frogs and Toads,* (1960), Charles A. Schoenknecht states on page 27, "Fish, turtles, herons, and other enemies eat many of the tadpoles. So only a small number of them live to be grown-ups." Perhaps the reader, alerted to the cue word "so", will want to explore just how many eggs are laid and what "a small number" means. Is the author's conclusion presenting a clear picture?

### GEORGE WASHINGTON LIES

One means of bursting the "anything that appears in print must be true" bubble is to have students read conflicting accounts of the same topic or incident. Try to determine reasons for discrepancies—author background, copyright date, and so on.

To help students understand how authors' backgrounds affect the way they write about an incident or event, have two students write individual stories or reports on the same topic (about a teacher or school event, for example). Note how each has chosen to focus on different aspects. It is possible that one report might even contain invalid statements.

With respect to copyright date, information in a book written prior to the first moon landing, for example, might state that human beings have never set foot on the moon. Since this contradicts what students have experienced to be true, they must question the information and try to discover why the inaccuracy exists, in this case because of when the material was written. The main point is that written material is not always accurate. This always comes as a surprise to some students.

## DO YOU AGREE?

Use popular sayings with which students agree or disagree, and have them provide reasons for their opinions. In this way, they may be shown the analytical skills that are a part of critical reading.

*EXAMPLES*      America is the land of the free.
Honesty is the best policy.

Aphorisms are another handy source material (e.g., the early bird catches the worm; a stitch in time saves nine).

## DO THE FACTS SUPPORT THE THESIS?

Use content or factual material with students to see whether the author has provided enough information to defend the topic sentence or concluding statements.

In *Reptiles Do the Strangest Things* (L. and A. Hornblow, 1970), the authors write that alligators sold as pets usually die and many crocodilians are killed for their skins, leaving the swamps depleted of these animals. They conclude by saying, "It is sad to think that the thundering 'song of the croc' may someday only be heard at the zoo" (p. 13), but they do not give reasons about why it is important to have crocodilians living in their natural habitat. Perhaps they are dangerous enough to man and do not provide enough value to the environment to justify the reader's feeling sad that they might soon only be found in zoos. This raises questions that students should at least ask when reading this book.

## COMMUNICATION

When authors put pen to paper (or fingers to keyboard), they are speaking to readers. Not only do they have something to say and a reason for expressing it, but their message is intended for a specific audience. Like the falling tree in the forest, their words need an ear. Authors write to inform, to entertain, to persuade, to teach or direct, and to express an idea or an emotion. Likewise, students read material for a variety of reasons; they may want to learn, be entertained, or find a new point of view, for example. Furthermore, both the author's and the reader's backgrounds will influence the resulting communication.

To illustrate the importance of both author and reader interaction, ask students to read several examples of different kinds of writing—a piece of fiction, an encyclopedia entry, an advertisement, a feature article in a newspaper, or a poem.

Have students answer from the following questions those which seem appropriate for each piece of writing suggested above:

Why is the author writing this? (What is the author's purpose?)
Why might a reader want to read this? (What is the reader's purpose?)
Why am I reading this? (What is *this* reader's purpose?)
Does the author's background make his/her message valuable?
For whom is the book written (i.e., for what audience?)?
Do readers need additional background knowledge to fully comprehend the message
Do I have the right background knowledge?
Is the message effectively and objectively presented?
Does this writing answer my question(s)?
Does this writing fit my mood?
Am I being influenced unfairly?

Asking students to write various pieces from different points of view and for different purposes helps illustrate the kinds of thinking an author uses when writing. If students are helped to recognize what is needed, they will be more open to thinking about these factors as they read.

## TO TELL THE TRUTH

In the early years of school, students read a great deal of fantasy. Animals in many stories dress and communicate like humans and often perform impossible feats. Although most students readily recognize that what they are reading is not real—monkeys don't talk in real life, even if Curious George does—there are finer distinctions of reality that students should be encouraged to note. Much of the message and many of the characters' actions and thoughts in fictional stories (fantasy as well as realistic fiction) are real. Students might analyze stories to discover which aspects are real and which are fantasy.

To illustrate how elements of reality are usually a part of fiction, demonstrate at the board a familiar story such as The Three Pigs (1970), charting incidents of character and plot.

| *Reality* | *Fantasy* |
| --- | --- |
| a mother leaving her children alone and telling them not to let anyone in | pigs speaking English |
| brothers disagreeing and each doing his own thing | pigs building homes with front doors and chimneys |
| brick is stronger than mud or straw | a wolf blowing a house down |
| one brother can be more sensible than the other two | a wolf knowing to enter a house by the chimney |
| boiling water can injure badly | pigs putting a pot of boiling water in the fireplace |
| brains can overcome physical strength and size | pigs outwitting wolves in the manner related |
| it often doesn't pay to take the easy way out | |

Fact and fiction intermingle in other ways as well. Although a plot and characters may be fictitious, the historical and geographical information can be fact. Robert Lawson's *Ben and ME* (1939) relates real events from Benjamin Franklin's life as seen by a mouse. *Make Way for Ducklings* (Robert McCloskey, 1941) describes factual territory familiar to anyone living in the Boston area, and yet ducks in the story talk and act in ways that we normally attribute only to humans.

Finally, we can designate works as primarily fact or fiction. Comparing two books on the same topic, one factual and one fiction such as Charles P. Graves' *Benjamin Franklin, Man of Ideas* (1960) and Lawson's *Ben and ME*, can help students to recognize the differences and to appreciate the advantages of each.

**I Believe That Is a Fact**

1. To illustrate differences between factual statements (those that can be proven true or false) and opinions (statements based on feelings or attitudes), look around the classroom and have students supply facts and opinions, discussing their identifying characteristics.

*EXAMPLES*    We can write on the blackboard.
            We think the blackboard is large.

Although a good hint about whether or not a statement is fact or opinion is to have students check for words that usually signify opinion (*appear, believe, could, think, seem, perhaps, probably, possibly, in all likelihood*), sometimes these words are included in factual statements.

*EXAMPLE*    The kindergarten children at Franklin School believe that the world is flat.

Statements containing adjectives related to quality (beauty, etc.) rather than quantity (a number), general statements, and those containing emotion-laden words are apt to be opinions. But often remarks can be considered as either fact or opinion.

*EXAMPLES*    Our high school is the best in the state.
            Cancer researchers have made great strides in the last ten years.

2. Students should recognize that author-stated opinions do not necessarily equal bad writing. Some opinions are based on fact and are worthy of note; others are totally unsubstantiated. Students need to make judgments about the merit of opinions after recognizing that a statement is indeed an opinion.
3. Writing up an incident both as a news story and as an editorial to make a point, helps students to understand the differences between fact and opinion, and highlights examples of their use. For example, a news story about a high school student who was killed when driving drunk would focus on the facts of the story, while an editorial on the same topic would more likely stress the unfortunate consequences of drinking and driving.

## WORD POWER

An author's purpose in writing determines the kind of language used. When the object is to entertain or amuse the reader, the writer may play with words or make use of puns as in Amelia Bedelia stories (Parish). When the purpose of the writing is to persuade, language with good and bad connotations is used. Advertisements are good examples of the use of persuasive language. (See Namecalling later in this section; also see Chapter 6 for a discussion of denotative and connotative meanings).

1. Have students write alternative ways of saying things to show the power of language in influencing feelings.

*EXAMPLE*

The child left.
The pouting, whining brat left.
The adorable angel of a girl left.
The nice young lady left.

Discuss the reactions of readers to the various versions supplied. Show how certain words evoke predictable emotions or feelings and that authors use these words intentionally. In *Reptiles Do the Strangest Things* (Hornblow, 1970), the authors Leonora and Arthur Hornblow comment, "Only one kind of reptile carries his house on his back. That is the wonderful turtle" (p. 28). The use of the word *wonderful* immediately identifies the writers' bias and certainly can be an influence on how readers of this chapter henceforth regard turtles.

2. Ask students to bring in menus from a number of restaurants. Show how the language used in the descriptions of the same dish can affect a diner's perception, and consequently, the desire to order a particular offering.

## YOU CAN FOOL SOME OF THE PEOPLE . . .

Acquaint students with well-known propaganda techniques. Those usually cited are:

1. *Namecalling:* Using a label without substantiating facts for a person or a product, the author hopes the connotation of the label will transfer. "Glad names" (She's a beautiful person) or "bad names" (She's a gossip) may be used.
2. *Testimonials:* Using celebrities to endorse ideas, people, or products, the author hopes the appeal of the celebrity rather than his or her expertise will sell the product. Well-known sports figures are used for numerous food and automobile advertisements.
3. *Transfer:* Similar to testimonials, a respected object or symbol (the American flag, for example) is used with a product in the hope that feelings for the object will transfer to the product.
4. *Bandwagon effect:* When readers are told everybody's doing it, they feel they too must join the crowd. This is a technique espoused by most teenagers when dealing with their parents.
5. *Plain folks:* The writer is appealing to the common man. A political candidate might speak of himself as "a man of the people."
6. *Card stacking:* Statistics are presented in a manner that favors a desired conclusion. "Four out of five doctors whose patients chew gum prefer Chew-Rite." The general impression is that four-fifths of all doctors, are represented whereas perhaps only one in ten of all doctors or four out of the five doctors they have selected are represented.

7. *Glittering generalities:* No hard facts support the thesis. "This car is spectacular. You'll feel wonderful driving the new Cosmos. Buy it!" "What is spectacular about it?" we hope students will ask. And how could a car be spectacular anyway? Have kids look up the meaning of spectacular and see if it could describe a car.

Having students identify television or newspaper and magazine ads that use these techniques helps them to recognize the techniques more deftly in the future. Writing ads for imaginary products demands that students understand the emotions and attitudes to which they are appealing.

As with opinions, not all propaganda is bad, but students should be aware of when it is used so that it they may intelligently decide to accept or reject what is advocated. Although there is no guarantee that understanding propaganda techniques will ensure that students can resist them, it is our hope that increased awareness will lead to stronger defenses as well.

# Activities to Go

**Propaganda Points**

SKILL: Critical reading

MATERIALS: Game board, sentence cards

PROCEDURE:
1. A student picks a propaganda sentence card (examples follow).
2. The student identifies the techniques used in the propaganda written on the card and adds the number of points indicated on the board.
   Example: Everyone knows that *Candyloo* is good for you. (4 [Bandwagon] + 7 [Glittering Generalities] = 11). Any reasonable answer can be accepted.
3. The next student picks a card, figures out the points for the card, and the two students compare point results. The player with the higher score gets a point and play continues until the cards are used. The one with the most points wins. (If more than two students are playing, points are compared after each player has taken a turn.)
4. A single student may wish to go through all of the cards and see which card uses the most techniques or earns the most points.

## SENTENCES FOR CARDS

1. The bounce of a real winner—buy the basketball the hometown team loves.
2. If Smellproof deodorant is good enough for heads of state in tense negotiations, then you know it's right for you.
3. All over the country people are saying, "It's Bonzo for me!"
4. Our all new liquid cleanser is 50% more effective.
5. The active ingredient in Glowy helps your dishes look terrific.
6. We may be small town folks but honesty is our trademark. When we say Hare is the best car available, we are telling the truth.
7. Whereas the cost of gas has increased 400% in the last twenty years, Blossom orange juice is up less than one-half of that.
8. For a sexy new look, use Curl-lash mascara.
9. Tired of looking ordinary? Players' clothes will make people sit up and take notice.
10. John Doe, the fast Olympic runner in 1992, runs for his Eatums each morning. A better breakfast cereal can't be found.

VARIATION: Have students search magazines for actual ads and see which products collect the most points.

# PROPAGANDA POINTS

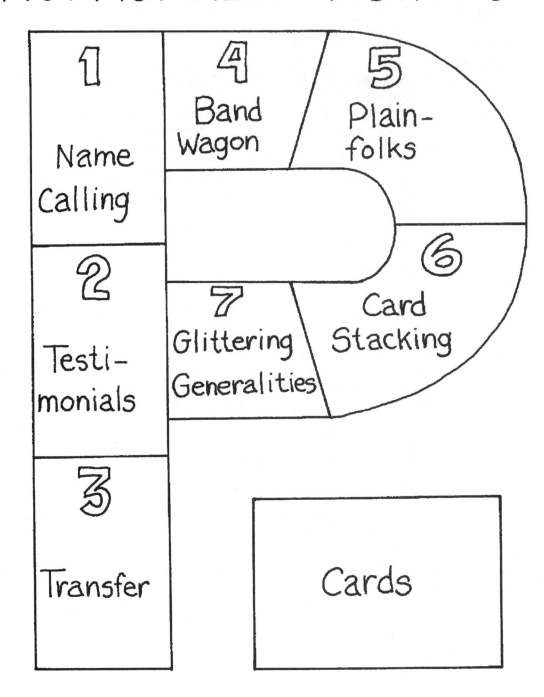

1 Name Calling

4 Band Wagon

5 Plain-folks

2 Testi-monials

7 Glittering Generalities

6 Card Stacking

3 Transfer

Cards

**Is That a Fact?**

Distinguishing fact from opinion

MATERIALS: Game board, sentence cards, board markers

PROCEDURE:
1. Two cards each containing a fact or opinion sentence are placed on each space. The sentence side is facing up. The word *fact* or the word *opinion* is written on the reverse side.
2. The two students begin at start and move one space at a turn. The student reads the sentence card and identifies the sentence as fact or opinion. The reverse side of the card reveals the answer (fact or opinion).
3. If the student is correct, she receives a point. Students alternate turns. The student with the most points at the end wins.
4. Optional—After deciding whether the sentence is factual or not, the student changes it into an opinion if it was a factual sentence or vice versa and wins a second point. "That racing car has been clocked at 100 miles an hour," may become: "I'll bet that racing car can go 100 miles an hour."

SENTENCES FOR CARDS:

See variation for "The _____ Have It! (Yeas or Nays" for ten sentences.

OTHERS:

*Facts:*

Susan is wearing a red dress.
I have a cut finger.
It is a Fall day.
John is President of the class.
Margie read a book.
Tim got an A in history.

*Opinions:*

Mary looks very good.
John Doe is certain to win the election.
It's hard to believe the year is half over.
He's gotten so big.
That is a thick book.
The car needs washing.

VARIATIONS: Cards for any skill may be used with this board. Written answers, if applicable, are placed on the reverse of each card.

# IS THAT A FACT ?

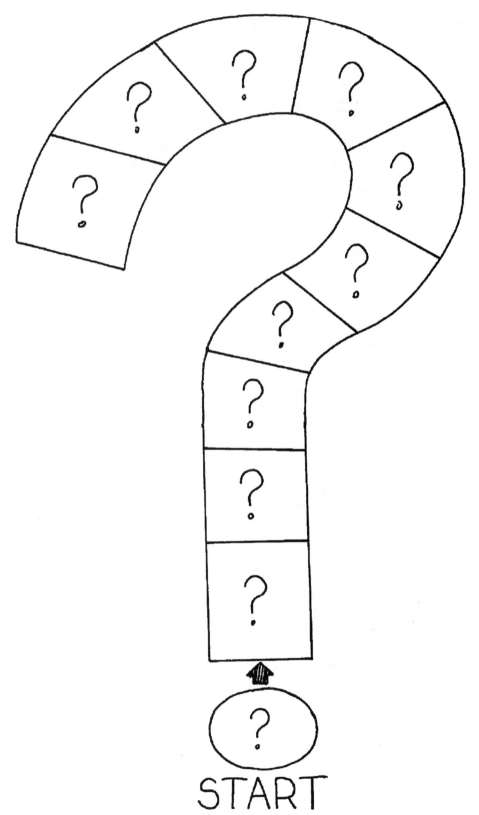

START

# 10
# Literary Concepts

Comprehending literature takes some special preparation. When students are about to read a piece of literature, whether story, article, poem, or play, helping them to remember both what they already know about that type of literature as well as the content of the particular piece will help them to better understand and appreciate it. Then providing lively and informative contexts in which students can share what they know and like about a piece of literature will help them to broaden their comprehension and enjoyment of literature.

Literature has conventions. Understanding these conventions helps students to form strategies that allow them to better understand and appreciate what they read. An awareness of the predictable narrative patterns in stories involves more than an understanding of the individual sentences. Students need to know that a story has a beginning, a middle, and an end. More specifically, narratives have (1) a setting, (2) character(s), (3) precipitating event or problem, (4) attempts to solve the problem, (5) a climax, and (6) a conclusion.

Two well-known stories can by analyzed this way—*Caps for Sale* (Slobodkin, 1947) and *Bread and Jam for Frances* (Hoban, 1964):

| *Caps for Sale* | *Bread and Jam for Frances* |
|---|---|
| (1) It's a beautiful day in the country. | (1) Inside the well-appointed Badger family residence. |
| (2) A cap salesman who is having a bad day, goes for a walk and then falls asleep under a tree. | (2) Frances, a badger child, is a picky eater who likes only bread and jam. |
| (3) While he sleeps, monkeys in the tree snatch all but one of the caps piled on the salesman's head. | (3) Mom Badger tries reverse psychology and offers only bread and jam at every meal. |
| (4) The salesman wakes up, shakes first one fist, then both, one leg, then both while shouting at the monkeys to return his caps. The monkeys shake their limbs right back, but don't return the caps. | (4) At first, Frances is happy about bread and jam at every meal. But her interest in food variety is piqued by a gourmet friend and a food-adventurous baby sister. |
| (5) In exasperation, the salesman throws his remaining cap to the ground. | (5) Finally, Frances breaks into tears at a family dinner when she is served a jam sandwich. |

(6) The monkeys, in imitation, throw the snatched caps to the ground. The salesman retrieves them and saunters back to town.

(6) Mom serves Frances the family's meatballs and spaghetti, and Frances finds that she likes it.

It should be mentioned that not all stories, especially those from non-Western European traditions, will have all of the aspects of story structure described above. For example, many stories from Latin cultures have no climax and resolution, but instead, a series of episodes serves as plot structure.

Additional literary conventions are in evidence in children's stories. Every story has a point of view, which is revealed through its narrator. Many stories contain figurative language, a tone, and/or a theme. A definition of each with an example follows:

- *Point of view*—This involves the story narrator. When a story is told by one of the characters, it is a first-person narration. *Alexander and the Terrible, Horrible, No Good, Very Bad Day* (Viorst, 1972) is a well-known story with a first-person narrator. When a story is told by someone other than a character, it is a third-person narration. *Miss Rumphius* (Cooney, 1982) is told by a third-person narrator. And when a story is told from several points of view, it has an omniscient narrator. *Dr. DeSoto* (Steig, 1982) has an omniscient narrator—you can view the action through the eyes of different characters at different points in the story.
- *Figurative language*—This is language that goes beyond a literal meaning to give a story a special feeling or effect. It usually compares one thing to another to achieve a particular image. Similes (She's as busy as a bee), metaphors (She's a real bee!), and personification (That day the sun was a bee with a butter knife, spreading popcorn-yellow light from flower to flower.)
- *Tone/Mood*-Tone and mood reveal an author's attitude toward his or her chosen topic. Characterization, setting, vocabulary, rhythm, rhyme, and style can all contribute to the achievement of tone or mood. Humorous, ironic, serious, or formal tones, and angry, joyous, or quiet moods can be found in children's literature.
- *Theme*—Many themes are really implied topics. A theme comprises the ideas and opinions behind a story, and is usually the author's reason for writing it in the first place. Aesop's fables have themes stated as morals. Rich literature will have many themes. *Little Women*, for example, has themes of family loyalties, personal growth and independence, war and sacrifice, and the search for love.
- *Genre*—Knowledge of literary conventions can expand students' understanding and appreciation of what they read. So too can an understanding of literary genres. A literary genre is a category of composition marked by a distinctive style, form, and/or content.

  In modern fantasy, for example, animals are often used in place of people to deal with intimate and urgent issues. The use of animals allows readers to identify with these issues, yet not feel threatened by overly personal content. So in these stories, animals often wear clothes, live in houses, go to school, and talk back to their parents!

  Fairy tales usually have people , very often royalty, as characters. It is the youngest or most vulnerable character in the tale who overcomes a problem that allows for living" happily ever after." The number three or seven may play an important role in a fairy tale as can the intervention of magical characters or forces of nature.

A final example is provided by historical fiction, in which characters inhabit an authentic setting from the past. While the setting, situations, and some characters may be real, the dialogue is invented and the events enhanced.

Other genres in children's literature include nonfiction, plays, poetry, biography, realistic fiction, science fiction, folk tales, tall tales, and fables. Each of these genres has conventions that you can make apparent to students as they read several examples .

## IDENTIFYING THE SKILL NEED

Both developmental stage and the type of literature at hand influence when students will need various literary skills. Students will benefit from an early introduction to the drama, for example, because they are learning that text is "talk written down," and, indeed, plays comprise just that—dialogue.

On the other hand, irony doesn't make sense as an early skill, because young readers are just beginning to grasp literal meanings and obvious humor. Symbolism, too, doesn't make sense for the early grades, since the alphabet and letter-sound relationships are a sufficient load of abstraction to be learned at that level.

Teaching the literary skills needed to comprehend the literature at hand seems obvious. Selecting literature for its quality and for its interest to students is a primary goal. Once the literature is selected, its special comprehension requirements may warrant attention to literary conventions and genres.

When Aesop's fable "The Tortoise and the Hare" is taught at first or second grade, students may not be able to fully appreciate the moral of the tale, but to exclude it from instruction would be a missed opportunity. Some students may be ready, while others can have exposure to the concept of moral, yet not be held directly accountable for it. Similarly, when Aesop's "The Wind and the Sun" is taught at those grades, a beginning level discussion of personification makes sense, even if you don't use the term itself.

## TEACHING THE SKILLS: TECHNIQUES AND ACTIVITIES

Strategies, techniques, and activities aimed at increasing students' appreciation and comprehension of literature focus on introductory activities, ways for students to respond to literature, and techniques for improving recognition and knowledge of literary conventions and genres.

### INTRODUCING LITERATURE

It has become accepted knowledge that as we read, we interact with the text to construct meaning. Some degree of background knowledge is needed in order for students to relate to literature in a meaningful way. By activating these background experiences when students approach a new text, they are better able to become actively involved with what they read: to make predictions, recognize esoteric vocabulary or terms, and evaluate the literature both critically and aesthetically. Below are suggestions that are often recommended for helping students bring their relevant prior experiences to the forefront.

### Semantic Mapping

Semantic mapping, described in Chapter 6 as a way of developing vocabulary, may also be used to help students organize what they already know about a piece of literature. It is useful for both narrative and expository text.

For example, in *Hattie the Backstage Bat* (Freeman, 1988), the word *theater* might be chosen to map or brainstorm associations. Words that students might volunteer, such as *audience, applause, rehearsal, stage, props,* and *actors* will provide them with an adequate background for understanding *Hattie,* especially since all of those words actually appear in the story!

### KWL

Activating background knowledge often helps students to establish a purpose for reading. This technique, which has students list everything they Know about the topic, everything they Want to know, and finally everything they've Learned, is especially effective for nonfiction.

### Anticipation Guides

Anticipation guides are also best suited to nonfiction. Students repond to a number of statements, which they designate as true or false. This technique has a number of benefits: It forces students to examine what they know about the subject in order to evaluate what they will read; it can introduce new vocabulary in helpful context; and it helps students to focus on the main ideas of the text. Like KWL, it both establishes purposes for reading as students read to verify their assumptions, and helps to clear up misconceptions.

An example of an anticipation guide for an article on kangaroos might have statements like:

1. Kangaroos are usually found in Europe.
2. Kangaroos move by leaping with their strong hind legs.
3. Baby kangaroos are called joeys.
4. There are different kinds and sizes of kangaroos.
5. Kangaroos are slow-moving animals.

### Compare and Predict

Have students think about other stories or texts on the same topic and try to predict how the current text might differ. When students make predictions, it may be necessary as they read to shift gears when the information in the text makes their prediction untenable. Using the textual information, they see that they need to make a new prediction. It may be necessary for you to model for the students how you do this as you read.

### I Wonder

Ask students after reading the title and perhaps looking at the pictures to think of three "I wonder" statements: "I wonder who . . .", "I wonder what . . ." and "I wonder where . . . ." Students then read to find the answers to their questions.

**Show Me**
When students lack sufficient background knowledge, it may be useful to use videos, television programs, field trips, classroom "re-enactments," maps, diagrams, or other relevant material to help fill in gaps prior to reading literature.

## RESPONDING TO LITERATURE

**Story Grammar Questions**
To help your students incorporate story grammar into their awareness of how stories unfold, you may wish to have your questions follow story grammar patterns as you review the plots of narratives your students read. For example, with the story *Hattie the Backstage Bat* (Freeman, 1988), your questions might be:

> Where does the story take place?
> Who is the main character? Who are the other characters?
> What is the problem?
> Find places where you think Hattie was tempted to disobey Mr. Collins's warning to stay out of sight.
> How did Hattie finally resolve the problem of staying out of sight?
> How did the story end?

If you follow this pattern each time that you discuss a story, students will begin to anticipate story sequence and hopefully will be looking for these elements.

**Story Grammar Summaries**
Summarizing stories is particularly difficult for most students. Often their summaries are longer than the stories themselves, as students get bogged down in details. A useful technique has students form a summary by answering four questions with one or two sentences for each. The questions follow the story grammar elements.

- When and where does the story take place and who are the characters?
- What is the problem?
- How is the problem resolved?
- How does the story end?

A summary of *Hattie the Backstage Bat* (Freeman, 1988) following this formula might be as follows:

> A bat named Hattie lived in an empty theater where the only person around was Mr. Collins, the janitor, who kept her company. When at last a play was booked for the theater, Mr. Collins made Hattie promise to stay hidden. But the night the play opened, Hattie was so excited she flew across the stage, casting a gigantic scary shadow. Since the play was about a bat, the audience loved it! From then on, Hattie performed every night.

**Journals**
Responding to literature in journals gives students the opportunity to react in very personal ways to their reading. Writing in journals can take many forms. Students may be invited to react to any aspect of their reading that they wish to. Or you may ask students simply to react to the plot, characters, or language of what they've

read. Or you might ask them to expand on the literature they've read by writing a new ending, telling the story from a different character's point of view, or describing how a character might react to another situation.

The kind of journal you ask students to keep may also vary. In a dialogue journal, students write to you about their reading and you write back, applauding their efforts and then prodding them to think about something they may have missed or that you'd like them to consider. Private journals allow for full freedom of expression while partner journals may be an aspect of partner reading with a peer.

### Literature Groups

These are groups composed of students who are reading the same book and meet to discuss it. These groups often are heterogeneous, comprised of students of different abilities who have a shared interest in a particular book. Sometimes the groups are homogeneous for reading ability.

Although you will monitor these groups, you may choose to let the students take charge of the discussion. You may wish to spend the first part of the year with the whole class modeling appropriate responses and questions for the literature groups.

You might schedule mini-lessons on setting, plot, character, language, or other relevant topics throughout the year, developing questions to be explored in literature groups and/or journals.

### Conferences

Scheduling individual conferences with students allows you concentrated time to help them understand and enjoy literature. During the conference time you may ask students to read aloud and comment on a favorite part of the story, read to you from their journals, talk about the characters, vocabulary, or any other aspect that you want students to focus on. If instruction is needed, this offers a ready opportunity.

### Literary Conventions

Many of the most effective techniques for helping students understand litarary conventions ask them to write. When students become authors themselves, they gain insight into the elements that comprise an interesting setting, plot, or characters.

- By having students rewrite a story changing the setting, they must think about whether the original setting worked for the plot and theme. In making a change, they will have to consider how the new setting affects these and other aspects of the story and will have to accommodate accordingly.
- Students' understanding of how point of view shapes a story is strengthened when you ask them to tell the story from the viewpoint of a different character

- By changing the beginning or the ending of a story or by adding another episode, students grapple first hand with aspects of plot.
- For a story that goes back and forth in time, having students tell the story sequentially helps them decide how flashbacks are an effective literary mechanism.

- Rewriting a story as a folktale or a fairy tale, changing poetry to prose, or making a short story into a play gives students many insights into these literary genres.
- By changing adjectives and/or the formality of the language, students can alter the mood of the story.
- Modeling the writing of a story after a particular book acquaints students with author style. Pattern books such as *Brown Bear, Brown Bear, What Do You See?* (Martin, 1983) are particularly well-suited to this.
- Similes, metaphors, personification, irony, hyperbole, and understatement are all understood more easily when students read, if they have had practice using them in their writing.
- Reading books on the same theme or books about similar characters and discussing both the similarities and the differences using a Venn diagram helps students understand literary conventions and genre. Venn diagrams can also help students also make connections between a book and their lives. The Venn diagram below shows how two stories, *Make Way for Ducklings* (McCloskey, 1941) and *The Story about Ping* (Flack, 1933), can be compared to each other and to the lives of children.

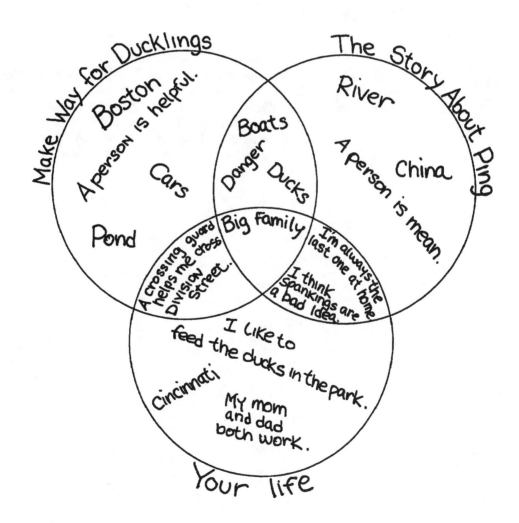

### Characters

Help students recognize that characters are often cast as heroes and villains. Construct with the class character charts of good and bad characters with appropriate examples from the text to defend the classification. Students may find that characters are both good and bad within the same text.

Have students understand the role that minor characters play in stories by telling how the stories would be different without these characters.

Encourage students to identify with characters by having them:

- Choose a character they would like to be.
- Write to characters to ask questions or give advice.
- Write to authors to ask about aspects of the characters that the book did not reveal, but that they would like to know about.

Help students to recognize the stock characters in different genres. For example, have them find the witches of fairy tales and the larger-than-life heros in tall tales.

### Mood and Tone

Have students identify stories where the mood is playful but the tone is serious to help them distinguish between the two. *The Butter Battle Book* (Seuss, 1984) provides a good example.

### Genre

To help students understand the characteristics of a particular genre, have students read a number of books in that category. Find the similar aspects, make charts with appropriate labels (e.g., Fables: animals representing human qualities, single episode, moral) and fill in the chart with each type of text read.

All books classified as fantasy or realism have both real/believable and fantastic/unbelieveable elements. Make a chart with students to show the realistic/fantastic or believable/unbelievable aspects of a story that they are reading.

# Activities to Go

**Story Shapes**

SKILL: Understanding story grammar

MATERIALS: Game board, marker

PROCEDURE:
1. Have students place the events of a story into either diagram or shape on the game board.
2. The train shape is appropriate if skill to be practiced is beginning–middle–end.
3. The staircase is designed to contain the five-part narrative structure—background, problem, attempts to solve it, climax, and resolution.
4. The completed shapesdemonstrate how the diagrams work.

## STORY SHAPES

Mon and woman baked a gingerbread boy.

He ran away from them, and then away from a hen, a duck, a goat, a dog.

But he could not run away from the fox, who ate him.

Finally the last and biggest goat challenged the troll to try to eat him

The first two billy goats tricked the troll who attempted to eat each one.

They had to cross the bridge to get to the hill to eat.

3 billy goats lived by a Troll's bridge.

The third goat Knocked the troll in the water.

*VARIATIONS:* **a.** Sometimes a central character can suggest a unique story shape. Two examples follow, but you'll need to create your own, given the particular stories your students read. Don't worry about lack of artistic gifts. Just trace a book illustration, as we did. Then write something about or from the story around or within the character shape.

**b.** For inferential comprehension, write a sentence in the middle of the train or on a step of the staircase and have students fill in logical sentences to precede and follow it.

---

*A tip of the hat to Dorothy Grant Hemmings, *Communication in Action: Teaching the Language Arts*, Boston: Houghton Mifflin, 1982.

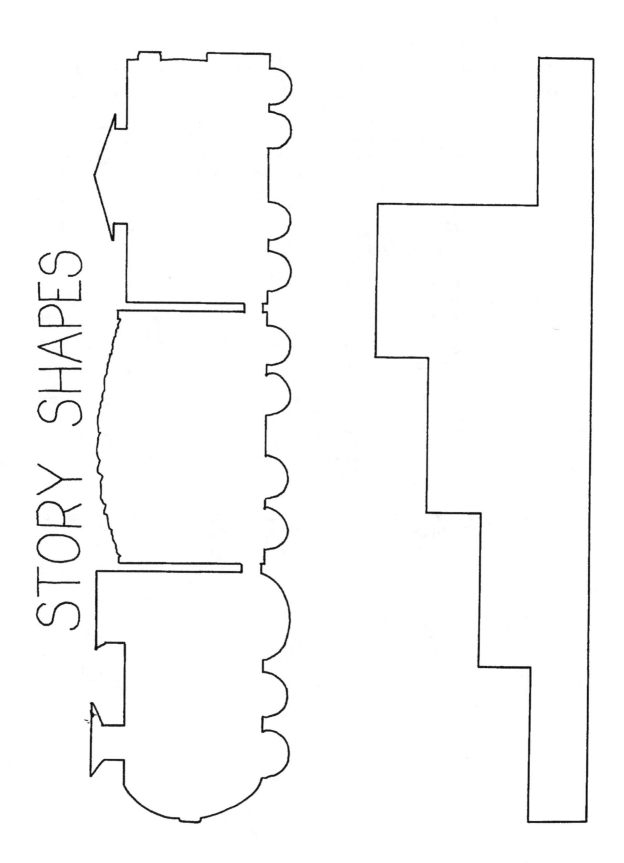

STORY SHAPES

119

*NAME:* **Characters**

*SKILL:* Literary analysis

*MATERIALS:* Game board, character trait cards, literature currently being read, markers

*PROCEDURE:*
1. Player place their markers on the "C" at the start of the game and move through each letter of the word CHARACTERS.
2. The first player picks a card. Each card has a character trait written on it. The player tries to find a character from the book for whom this trait is appropriate.
3. If the player can justify this match of character and trait with specifics from the text, the player moves to the next letter ("H") and it is now the next player's turn.
4. Play continues until the players reach the last letter of the word CHARACTERS.

*CHARACTER TRAIT CARDS:*

| | |
|---|---|
| clever | industrious |
| fearful | cautious |
| generous | kind |
| angry | loving |
| stingy | neat |
| articulate | cheerful |
| mean | grouchy |
| adventurous | considerate |
| foolish | trusting |
| grateful | friendly |
| curious | caring |
| lazy | humble |
| witty | optimistic |

*VARIATION:* If there are enough characters in a particulary story, assign one to each letter of the word CHARACTERS. Then play the game as instructed.

**121**

# 11

# Obtaining and Remembering Information from Text

In order to do well in school, students must demonstrate that they have learned the concepts and facts of a subject, and can apply this knowledge. Special strategies are required for gathering information from printed sources, and, for those of us without photographic memories, additional strategies help us remember the information. These strategies are called study skills.

The study skills we use vary according to specific tasks. In textbook reading, distinguishing the literal main idea from supporting details requires perusal of headings and topic sentences. On the other hand, the creation of a category that encompasses the details of a selection is necessary in the case of an inferred main idea. To store the main idea for later use, readers may make use of a written summary paragraph. However, to retrieve the details during a test, acronyms can help. (e.g., FACE identifies the notes in the spaces of printed music while the phrase "*Every good boy does fine*" helps us remember the notes on the lines.)

Other abilities, those that help students make use of reference materials, are included among the study skills. Dictionaries, encyclopedias, atlases, and almanacs, while not strictly classroom materials, demand special reading techniques.

We have limited the strategies in this chapter to those associated with learning from text. Omitted are those necessary for taking lecture notes, budgeting time, or writing a term paper. Certainly these are important skills, but they are less directly related to reading. Those we do discuss are divided into three categories: (1) information-gathering processes such as outlining, (2) storage techniques such as summarizing, and (3) retrieval strategies, one of which is category structuring.

## IDENTIFYING THE SKILL NEED

In the primary grades, students read more stories than nonfiction. Because they often lack sufficient exposure to expository text, middle grade students may have difficulty understanding this type of writing. This difficulty may be largely responsible for the "third-grade dip" that students experience in reading achievement and interest.

Expository writing is more difficult in some ways. Its content is more objective, and students often lack the background of experiences that would ease comprehension. Vocabulary and concept load is usually denser than than that found in fiction. In addition, students must work harder at understanding how information is organized. For example, while most stories follow a temporal sequence, history texts follow both temporal and cause-and-effect sequences.

The kind of reading instruction most often associated with fiction is directed or guided reading. Students are often given extensive concept-building and vocabulary instruction before they begin reading, oral questions as they read, and an opportunity for general discussion afterwards. Often students are able to select what they want to respond to. Therefore the written questions and chapter tests that accompany learning from textbooks in the middle grades place new skill demands on readers.

If you are a primary teacher, you would do well to prepare your students for the demands of expository writing by providing instruction in nonfiction and its special conventions as soon as reading instruction begins. And if you are a middle grade teacher, you have the bulk of responsibility for textbook reading instruction. But those of you who are upper grade and high school teachers may find that no one before you has done the job well enough. Although you would probably rather teach only what is in the textbooks for your subject, you may find yourself helping students learn how to read those textbooks as well.

## TEACHING THE SKILLS: TECHNIQUES AND ACTIVITIES

### INFORMATION GATHERING

**Laying Foundations**

Before students can outline a selection, they must be able to distinguish between its main idea and details. When authors include headings or topic sentences in textbook writing, finding main ideas and details is a literal skill. But such explicit information is often absent from expository writing, and main ideas often need to be inferred, usually by giving a category name to the details of a selection.

The following strategies will help students distinguish main ideas from details:

1.  *Telegrams*—This activity asks students to reduce the information in a selection to its essentials so that it may be sent in telegram form. Explain to students how much it costs to send a telegram and give them a budget to stick to. Let them see how details add needed clarity and sometimes essential data.

| | | |
|---|---|---|
| Cousin Denise and Aunt Fay expect to take the ten o'clock shuttle out of Dulles Airport and will arrive in Philadelphia at 10:52. Please pick them up at the airport. | @ 20¢ a word $2.20 | Denise and Fay taking 10 o'clock flight. Meet them at 10:52. |
| | @ 20¢ a word $1.20 | Meet Denise, Fay at airport 10:52. |

2. *Categories*—Give students lists of related words without their topic label, and ask them to supply it. Move on to related sentences that require a subheading and then to related paragraphs. Many teachers like to take newspaper articles or old basal stories and delete the title. An important adjunct to this activity is a discussion with students about the "why" of their choices. If possible, have them explain their reasoning, and if this proves difficult, explain your choice. Model your thinking processes for them.

a. _____(topic label goes here)
   setter
   poodle
   terrier
   shepherd

b. _____(title goes here)

   Some hypnosis is a condition of detachment. The everyday world fades and a new frame of reference becomes the focus of attention. An altered state of consciousness or trance results. Under another form of hypnosis, the subject seems asleep but can talk. In still other cases, the subject seems wide awake and even responds more quickly than usual.

3. *Names of . . .*—The reverse of "Categories," this oral activity, a kind of chant, asks students to come up with the probable details of a main idea. The chant has four beats: First the players slap their hands on their thighs. Next they clap their hands together. Finally, they snap their right-hand fingers and then their left. This series constitutes one round (slap, clap, snap, snap). While fingers snap during the first round, students recite "Concentration." During the second round of snaps, they chant "names of." With the third round, one student chooses a category, dogs. for example, and chants it during the snaps.

   Then the rhythm continues as each player in turn names a member of the category (setters, terriers, greyhounds). When a player fails to name one, he drops out of the game. The last player left is the winner.

### Building Outlines

Written outlines are particularly useful because they bridge the gap between all phases of study from information gathering to storage to retrieval. The outlining habit, too, is an excellent way to approach expository writing instruction.

Outlining should flow naturally from distinguishing main ideas and details. It takes many forms, most of which are quite similar. Of course, students and their teachers can use or create their favorites. We like using the initial letters of the main idea (MI) and detail (D) with subscripts to help remind student of the concept behind outlining:

MI 1
  D 1
  D 2
MI 2
  D 1
  D 2
  D 3

At first, outlines should be created from brief selections that have clearly stated main ideas found either in subheadings or topic sentences, and evident supporting details:

Gravity is a force that pulls everything toward the center of the earth. It is hard to lift a heavy package because gravity pulls it down. It is easier to run downhill with the help of gravity than it is to run uphill with gravity working against you. In fact, if it wasn't for gravity, you'd float off into space. Gravity is the force that allows us to keep our feet firmly planted on the earth.

To begin the instructional sequence in outlining, you may wish to present a completed outline to students, and then gradually withdraw the amount of information provided. If the selection above were used in a first lesson, the first outline below would be appropriate, the blank lines representing what students need to supply. Samples of what students would fill in during subsequent lessons follow the first outline.

M1_____

    D1 It makes heavy things hard to lift.

    D2 When you throw something up, it will come down.

    D3 Going downhill is easier than coming up.

    D4 It keeps us from floating away from the earth.

M1 Gravity pulls things to the center of the earth.

    D1 It makes heavy things hard to lift.

    D2 _____

    D3 Going downhill is easier than coming up.

    D4 _____

M1 _____

    D1 _____

    D2 When you throw something up, it will come down.

    D3 _____

    D4 _____

When the main idea is inferred, as in the next selection, students may be required to choose among sentences, phrases, or titles, and then eventually create them on their own.

Why not turn off a light if it's not in use? People can walk or use public transportation instead of driving everywhere. They can keep their house temperatures at a reasonable 67 degrees, and take a hot shower instead of a hot bath. Watching less television and reading more could save large amounts of fuel as well.

A. Choose the best topic sentence for the paragraph.
    1. Americans need more physical exercise.
    2. There are many steps to take to ease our fuel crisis.
    Good conservation habits start in the home.
B. Write a good title for the paragraph.

### What's in a Textbook?

The format of textbooks is relatively consistent across subject areas and grade levels—that is, there is usually a preface, a table of contents, an index, a glossary, and a list of references. To get the most from a text, students should make use of these aids.

Probably the most useful technique for teaching such skills consists of teacher-made questions about the text features of a particular book.

How can you answer these questions?

1. In what chapter can you find information about holidays? (Table of Contents)
2. Name 2 other books that you might look at to compare information about the treatment of heart disease. (Bibliography or References)
3. What pages in this text deal with adoption? (Index)

### How to Read a Textbook Chapter

Individual text chapters have a structural similarity that allows for a single approach for studying them. There have been many techniques created to help students extract information from text chapters. The best known of these approaches is SQ3R (Survey, Question, Read, wRite/Recite, Review). Our contribution to these systems is GRUNT (Guess what this chapter is about, Read to check your guesses, Uncover the truth, Notetake, Test yourself).

Most important about these systems is they give students something *active* to do when they approach texts and can bolster students' confidence about their probable success with the material. Moreover, like outlining, parts of the system are written and therefore can be stored for later retrieval.

In our experience, one difficult task for students is taking the content obtained from a survey of the chapter and turning it into questions or hypotheses to be confirmed by careful reading. Try one or two of these options with the subheading: The life cycle of a frog.

Option 1. Just place a question mark at the end of the statement: The life cycle of a frog?
Option 2. Place the words "What is" at the beginning of the statement: What is the life cycle of a frog?
Option 3. Create a cloze statement: The life cycle of a frog_____

### Graphically Speaking

Not only does the format of textbook chapters need special attention, but so do the graphic or visual aids that are plentiful in expository writing. Usually students have had picture-reading experiences, but most often the illustrations in children's stories present the information representationally—that is, with the objects and persons with which students are familiar. The visual aids in textbooks, however, often use symbolic visuals such as bar graphs, maps, and cross-sections. Instruction to gain facility with graphic aids is necessary for all readers. Here are some suggestions:

1. Use the students' interests and immediate environment as data for class-made visual aids. For example, make graphs of students' shoe sizes, pets, ball-team loyalties, and the like. Start with picture graphs, since those most closely resemble story illustrations, and then move ahead to bar and line graphs. Maps of the classroom, school block, or neighborhood should precede those of city, country, and continent.

2. To remove students one step from familiar contexts, have them make graphics that re-express information from familiar stories. Have them chart, for instance, how many siblings each of their favorite story characters has or diagram a floor plan of their favorite story-family's home.

3. Finally, though, students must deal with totally decontextualized graphics; little personal or story experience can be brought to bear on most textbook visuals. The following are some suggestions to make that task easier.

   • Explain to students how diagrams usually represent a portion of a whole. The diagram, which depicts how a steam engine works, is really a piece of the whole steam engine, and a cross-section at that. Moreover, scale considerations need to be noted.

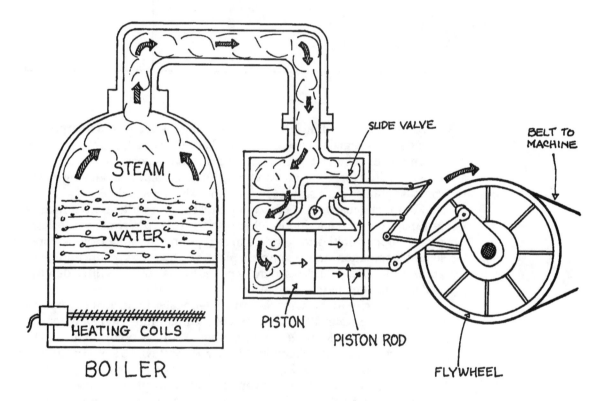

   • Tables are scanned differently from connected discourse. Row and column perusal need to be explained; otherwise, the untrained student may read the lines of chart titles straight across.

   • Reading quantitative measures such as circle graphs is best shown by use of the "pie technique." Get a pie or other three-dimensional circular object and divide it up. Then move to a cutout circle, and finally to a circle drawn on paper. Or take blocks and stack them in varied-size columns, one block representing each counted item. Then on a large piece of chart paper, trace the columns from the blocks. Finally, draw the bar graph directly on a smaller sheet of paper, reducing the column sizes proportionately.

   • Maps are, perhaps, the most difficult of all visual displays to comprehend because we never see the whole that the picture represents. As a consequence, many of us have an inner perception of the United States that looks very much like that puzzle map we worked on as children—pink, blue, and light green!

| KIND OF MODEL | SOURCE OF POWER | SPEED OF TRAVEL | | | DISTANCE OF TRAVEL (IN FEET) |
|---|---|---|---|---|---|
| | | FAST | MEDIUM | SLOW | |
| CAR | COILED SPRING | X | | | 35 |
| BOAT | RUBBER BAND | | | X | 10 |

Nevertheless, finding locations, measuring distances, and interpreting legends are essential map-reading tasks. Each map or atlas uses its own set of symbols or abbreviations that depend on what is portrayed on the map. However, lines for roads, dots and stars for cities, blue symbolizing water, compass points, and a scale of miles seem to be universal.

Comparing map types is a technique that allows students to compare a text map with those found in other sources, particularly atlases. Atlases provide opportunities to compare map types of the same region—topological, population, animal, human, plant, weather, and production maps are examples. Have students identify places by matching a written description to several maps of the same area:

1. Find a city in the southeastern United States in an area covered by standing water 10 to 50 percent of the time. You can travel there by car, south on Route 26. Many earthquakes have occurred there. The average family income in this city in 1959 was $4569. Its current population is about 79,500.
2. Compare wildlife and human population maps of Australia to see which animals live closest to big cities and which live in areas of sparse human habitation.
3. Compare a modern map of Israel with one of the same area during the reign of King David. Are cities in the same locations and have place names changed?

**Looking It Up**

In order to expand on information available in a text, it is necessary that students use reference books, particularly encyclopedias and dictionaries, along with other nonfiction sources. To make such books attractive for use, try introducing fun references first. *The Guiness Book of World Records, The Book of Lists, The Kids' Almanac,* and *The Baseball Almanac* are well-known sources. Also motivating and important to master are nonschool references such as the phone book, cookbooks, and *TV Guide.*

### Our Friend, Noah Webster

Special skills are necessary to make maximum use of a dictionary. Alphabetization usually comes to mind, for a word must be located before its definition can be read. You should be cautious about assigning too many actitivies for developing alphabetization. Being able to alphabetize to the second letter is probably sufficient for the efficient use of student dictionaries. A little time spent scanning up and down columns of words isn't lost if, in the process, students can uncover words they didn't (but always wanted to) know.

However when time is short, guide words can be helpful. Have students decide whether a particular word, let's say *heathen*, can be found on a page with certain guide words, let's say *heater* and *heather*. Then reverse the process and have students make up probable guide words for the page on which you would find the entry for *basket*. Explain the whys of right and wrong answers. Then require practice: (1) look up real entries and note the guide words, and (2) find actual guide-word pairs and note entries between them.

Once words can be found, the most important skill in using dictionaries is being able to distinguish among available definitions for any entry. Students can:

1. Provide illustrations for varied definitions of one word:

a run (in a stocking)

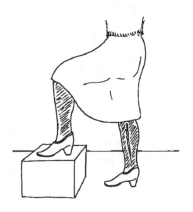

to run (for president)

to run (an elevator)

to run (move fast)

2. For an overused word in a text or composition, urge students to use synonyms located in a dictionary or thesaurus To exaggerate the result of word overuse, try a selection like this:

Too Much Niceness to Be Nice

One nice day, a nice man named Neil was waiting for his nice daughter Nancy in a nice park. Nancy had taken Neil's nice car and had gone to buy a nice dress. While waiting, Neil sat on a nice part bench to eat a nice lunch.

3. Play fictionary—Give students a sample dictionary entry with multiple definitions, one of which is false and has been created by you. See if your students can find the fictional definition by choosing what they think is the made-up definition and then checking their hypothesis with a dictionary.

EXAMPLE   *Stand*

(a) to be upright on your feet
Don't *stand* if you're tired.
(b) to attach
*Stand* these papers with a clip or staple.
(c) be in a certain place
Columns *stand* on either side of the door.
(d) a group of growing trees.
Choose your Christmas fir from that *stand*.

4. Give students sentences containing several meanings of a target word. Have them match each one to the appropriate dictionary definition.

| Sentence | | Definition | |
|---|---|---|---|
| a. | The horses *draw* the heavy wagon. | 1. | gather |
| b. | *Draw* fifty dollars from your bank account. | 2 | take out |
| c. | It's hard to *draw* conclusions from the little you know. | 3. | sketch |
| d. | That juggler can sure *draw* a crowd. | 4. | pull |
| e. | That artist can sure *draw* a crowd. | 5. | infer |

5. Let students discover the fun that dictionaries can be. When unabridged, dictionaries are multipurpose references. Foreign language sections, a list of given names with etymologies, atlases, and symbol dictionaries may hold fascination for students, along with those detailed engravings of esoteric machinery and rarely seen animals. Dictionaries *are* appropriate for recreational reading!

**Encyclopedias**

These reference books are often misused even by the best of students, who may be tempted to copy whole selections to use in classroom reports. Naturally, it is essential that students use their own words.

This is no small task for most elementary students. Encyclopedias are written at a level that makes them difficult to understand. If you wish to use them with your students, you may want to use the following sequence of instruction:

1. Start with report topics such as animals, since encyclopedia articles about them are relatively short and easy.
2. Require that students use the first person in their reports since it makes verbatim copying impossible. (I'm a Fiddler Crab, but I don't play the fiddle and I'm not crabby!)
3. Have students write down everything they already know about a topic, and everything they want to know.

   What I Know about Crabs          What I Want to Know about Crabs

4. Encourage students to improve on encyclopedia language by asking them to make their report much shorter and much more interesting than the encyclopedia version.
5. Allow students to report on only the most interesting facts.
6. It is also important to point out to students that encyclopedia content, though factual, is written by one author who sees the topic subjectively and for that reason is not the last or only word on the subject. Other references must be used with an encyclopedia. After students select a topic from an encyclopedia volume, have them go to a list of library holdings to find several sources on the same topic and compare information. What do the books tell that the encyclopedia does not and vice versa?

## STORING INFORMATION

After information from expository text has been gathered, it may be necessary to store it for a written report, oral discussion, or test. The storage techniques that follow have been shown to increase memory for text. Because retention is a highly individual matter, it may take a while to find the best-fitting method for each student. It is recommended that you ask students to describe, if possible, how they best remember something. You may want to give them several of the alternatives below as choices if they can't come up with something on their own.

**Outlines Before or After?**
Have students outline a selection (or give them your outline) in advance to learn it before they read. This technique has been shown to increase memory for details. If inferencing is the goal of instruction, giving an outline or requiring one from students after their reading is recommended.

**Highlight the Highlights**
Tell students in advance which are the important ideas in a selection they are about to read. Have them use sticky notes to mark important sections and write some ideas on the notes. Afterwards, have them reread the marked sections as many times as they like until they feel they know the material. A brief quiz will show students if the number of rereadings was enough for learning. Later, to gain more independence in this skill, students can decide what the important ideas are as they read, mark them, and in a discussion, get help in deciding if these are the most important ones after all.

**Note Taking**
The form of appropriate note-taking depends, in part, on the kind of material used. Students can mark directly in texts that they own or on xeroxed material. For school-

owned books, taking notes in a separate notebook, or using sticky notes makes sense. It seems wise to teach underlining or highlighting and marginal note taking so that students have a number of options. Whichever system is used, check notes that students have made to be sure that important ideas are noted and ancillary information is omitted. Because students often highlight information that interests them in addition to or instead of that which represents central thoughts, you may wish to require two-color ink or two-column notes—one color (column) for main issues, and another for personal interests.

If students use an outline or SQ3R to help with information gathering, the outline or written answers taken down during that process will serve as notes.

### Tell About It in Your Own Words
As an alternative to outlining, written summaries serve well as notes. Students may want to read as much as they can remember in one session, and then retell it in their own words.

Using a word processor is especially helpful in this way. Encourage students to read a little, input a little, read a little, input a little until they have a set of notes. Having put the ideas of the text into their own words makes it more likely that the content will be remembered, too!

### Seeing Aids Remembering
Have students form a visual image of events either in their heads or on paper. When descriptions are available, but illustrations are not, encourage students to form a mental image by closing their eyes and attempting to see the scene complete with action and dialogue! Even better, albeit more time-consuming, is a drawing of the scene.

### Our Thanks to the Spider
Another kind of visual image connects words in a diagram called a semantic web. Webs can increase memory for content by providing a framework or schema in which to house details. It is a specific physical arrangement that can later facilitate retrieval. If a selection topic were "summer food," relationships from the semantic map could be drawn several ways.

One could mention that sometimes fresh fruit is used in the creation of cold drinks. Grape or apricot juice, orange soda, and even that slice of lemon in iced tea show that connection. Popsicles, shish-kabob, and corn have similar shapes. The former two foods are prepared on a stick, but only the first is eaten on a stick. Seemingly limitless invention make this activity enjoyable as well as memorable.

### Slow Down

It is important for students to adjust reading speeds. This approach will be given more attention in the next chapter. Here it will be enough to say that studying is better done at a slower pace than recreational or normal classroom reading.

### Relate, If Possible

Have students attempt to assimilate content into their personal lives. Content area reading is usually perceived by students as quite removed from their lives. If you can create prereading activities that prepare students by tapping into their feelings and experiences, the subsequent reading will be more memorable.

### Spaced Learning

Putting time between attempts to learn from text seems to increase memory for it. This is probably because each study session takes place under slightly different personal and environmental conditions, thus creating multiple memories, one for each study attempt. When students later try to retrieve and one memory path is blocked, they can attempt another one.

### "Sensible" Learning

This suggestion is similar to spaced learning. Students attempt to remember content by feeding it to memory through several senses or modes. When students listen to the information as you or another student reads it aloud, or as they listen to a tape, aural access is provided. Reading about the information or seeing it on video or film provides visual access. Writing notes and outlines or answering study guide questions utilizes a kinesthetic pathway to memory. Finally, reciting the information aloud to oneself or to a studymate involves yet another communication mode—speaking. This may be the most effective channel, since it closely resembles teaching, a process we've found to be the best way to learn anything!

### RETRIEVAL

The last step in the sequence that begins with information gathering is called retrieval. This refers to the ability to gain access to information stored in memory.

Most strategies for retrieval fall under the heading "associations"—that is, the target information is compared to or associated with other data, usually more memorable or at least more personal than the target information. The more personalized data is joined with the target information during storage and later the former data is recalled first and pulls with it the targeted data.

At times, retrieval strategies are unplanned—students may remember a word because it was the longest one they learned in a particular lesson. However, planning retrieval strategies takes a bit more work.

If students anticipate the task of retrieval during their information gathering and storage sessions, they'll be halfway home; that is, planning for retrieval or setting up associations in advance is essential. Giving students examples of retrieval strategies is your job, but eventually students must find their own tricks, associations that work for them. Some strategies that have been useful for many students are:

### Spelling Tricks

These are good examples of planned retrieval strategies. A song like "Bingo" helps children spell one of their first words—B-I-N-G-O. "Look" is spelled with two o's, a fact made memorable by turning those o's into eyes that look out at the reader.

### Category Structures

To remember a list of words, store it with a category structure. This helps to narrow possible members of the list. For example, when you ask students experiencing word identification difficulty to remember that "it's a word that we had yesterday," you are calling to mind a category of items called "All the words we learned yesterday." That may not seem like much of a clue until you compare it with the categories "All we learned yesterday" or "All the words we learned last week."

### Numbers

To help narrow the field of what needs to be retrieved still further, knowing the number of items for recall is helpful. To remember the names of the New England states, it might help to first identify their number, six.

### Acronyms

Using the first letter of each detail to be recalled to form an acronym or other mneumonic can be helpful. ROY G. BIV helps us to remember the names of the colors in a prism or rainbow (red, orange, yellow, green, blue, indigo, and violet). HOMES reminds us of the Great Lakes (Huron, Ontario, Michigan, Erie, and Superior). Homemade mneumonic devices aren't as neat as ROY G. BIV, but they are equally or even more useful. If students were trying to remember the names of the New England states, they might store them with the number six, and perhaps, this phrase: M & M's RuN for CoVer. (The double M's are Massachusetts and Maine, the R and N are Rhode Island and New Hampshire, the Co is Connecticut, and the Ver is, you guessed it, Vermont!)

Although this may seem farfetched, the fact that students create the device makes it memorable and fun. The energy involved in the act of creating acronyms is often enough to imprint the information.

# Activities to Go

NAME: **Storm**

SKILL: Distinguishing main ideas from details

MATERIALS: Game board, markers

PROCEDURES: Storm is a game of categories that provides practice with generating details for a given main idea.

1. A five-letter word is written vertically in the left hand column of a 6 X 6 grid.
2. Categories are chosen and written across the top row.
3. Players, working on their own or in teams, write down members of the categories that begin with each letter at the left.
4. Be careful to select broad categories and words that do not repeat letters or have letters found infrequently at the beginning of a word. (*Quill* would be a bad choice.)

Scoring: Two points are given for each original word, one that other players haven't written down. One point is given if a word has also been used by another player.

CAUTION Do not expect students to fill in an entire grid.

## ←——CATEGORIES——→

| STORM | Dogs | Boys' names | Book Titles | Cities | Veggies |
|-------|------|-------------|-------------|--------|---------|
| S | Schnauzer | Sam | Sybil | Secaucus | Salad |
| T | Terrier | Terrace | To Think That I saw it on Mulberry St. | Teaneck | turnip |
| O | Otterhound | Ollie | Over Sea Under Stone | Oklahoma City | Okra |
| R | Retriever | Roger | Return of the Native | Reno | radish |
| M | mutt | Melvin | Madeline | Minneapolis | mushroom |

FIVE LETTER WORD →

VARIATIONS: Other good five-letter words: earth, glint, learn, sport, ranch, melts
Other categories: animals, flowers, ball teams, movies, cars, verbs, adjectives for food

# CATEGORIES

|  |  |  |  |  |  |
|--|--|--|--|--|--|
|  |  |  |  |  |  |
|  |  |  |  |  |  |
|  |  |  |  |  |  |
|  |  |  |  |  |  |
| STORM |  |  |  |  |  |

FIVE-LETTER WORD ←

**Study Skills Crossword**

SKILL: Study skills terminology

MATERIALS: Photocopy of puzzle, pencil

PROCEDURE:
1. Photocopy the puzzle.
2. Have students complete the puzzle in order to review what they have learned about study skills.
3. Invite students to compare their completed puzzle with the answer key below.

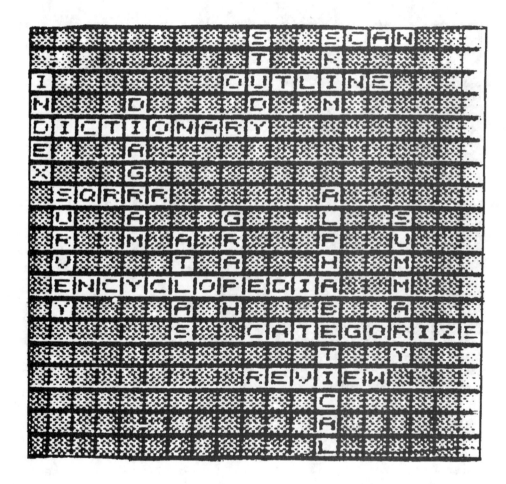

# STUDY SKILLS CROSSWORD

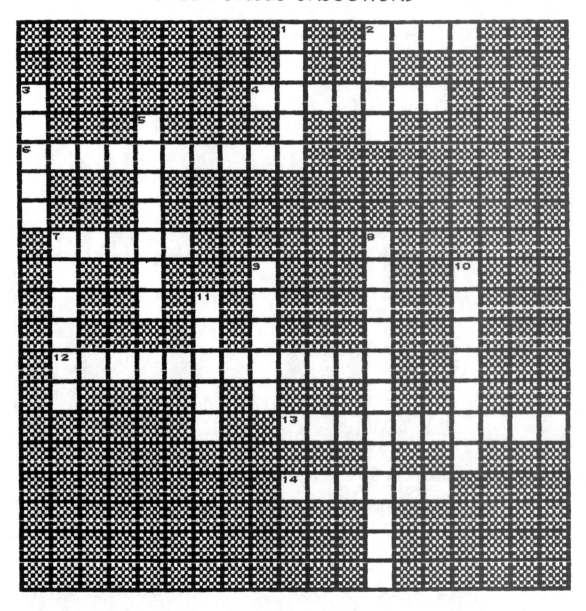

**Across Clues**

2. To read quickly to find a detail
4. Notes which show only the main ideas of a book or chapter
6. A book of the meanings and pronunciations of words
7. A system for the careful reading of a textbook chapter
12. A set of books with articles on many topics
13. To group like details together in order to remember them
14. Go over something again to refresh one's memory

**Down Clues**

1. Read carefully to try to learn something
2. To read quickly for the main ideas
3. An alphabetical list of the contents of a book
7. To get an overview of a textbook chapter
8. The order in which words can be found in a dictionary
9. A diagram which shows the relationship between two or more things by using dots, bars or lines
10. A brief statement of the main ideas of a book or chapter
11. A collection of maps

# 12

# Reading Rate

## DESCRIBING THE SKILL

When considering how fast or slow your students read, it's necessary to understand effective, or flexible, reading rates. Students with flexible rates use the following strategies: They slow down when they study and when they read difficult, unfamiliar material; they speed up when reading easy or familiar text, and when skimming, scanning, or reading recreationally.

Students with successful reading rates are almost always fluent readers. When reading aloud, especially from a familiar book, they can make written text sound like natural spoken language. When reading silently, they process text rapidly enough to facilitate comprehension.

Slow reading in all situations is often the result of immature, or poor, word analysis. When the need to decode each word puts primary focus on pronunciation, rate, or fluency, comprehension may suffer. Even when decoding is mastered, the slow rate picked up during that stage may remain and be utilized, whatever the reading purpose.

A consistently slow speed is one type of reading rate inflexibility. A consistently fast rate is another. Some students may read all texts at a fast rate, regardless of their difficulty or the students' familiarity with their contents.

## IDENTIFYING THE SKILL NEED

Beginning readers are at a stage of reading development in which they often need to stop and decode unknown words. Some beginners even attempt to decode words they can read instantly, because they are practicing newly learned decoding skills. We believe such a concentration on decoding to be perfectly reasonable, at least through third grade. Therefore, we believe it makes sense to wait until children achieve approximately fourth-grade reading ability before you instruct them in rate increase. On the other hand, fluency, or making reading sound like speaking, should be an instructional goal at all grade levels.

Generally, little classroom time is devoted to instruction in flexible rate, and most students seem to be convinced of the necessity of reading evey word. This may be true because oral reading is emphasized in the lower grades. But oral and silent reading speeds should differ, as soon as students can manage it. Silent reading should be faster than oral, because silent reading isn't dependent on pronunciation (reading aloud) or subvocalization (moving lips), processes that slow reading considerably. During an oral reading "performance," every word counts. For silent reading, however, skills like skimming, or even skipping (because you know the content, or because it's boring) make sense.

Once students are taught to skim, scan, or skip portions of text, however, some of them overuse these techniques. For example, students may skim stories or chapters that need in-depth processing. Sometimes students who are given comprehension questions before a story read only those sections of it that supply the answers. While this may be appropriate behavior when taking a test, it is limiting when applied to other reading situations.

## TEACHING THE SKILLS: TECHNIQUES AND ACTIVITIES

### FLUENCY FIRST

Through cooperative or paired reading, slower readers may be moved along by faster readers. And if you read with the students in a shared reading experience, the group as a whole will be moved along at your pace. In addition, when you read aloud to your students, you provide them with a model of fluency.

### READING IT AGAIN

Reading fluency is aided when texts are easy and familiar to students. One way texts become familiar is to have students read them again and again. As students reread a story, either because they enjoy it, or because they want to commit it to memory, their reading will become increasingly more fluent.

### READING IN IDEA UNITS

Segment a portion of written discourse into idea units. These are words generally phrased together when read aloud, or held together by punctuations or by phrase or clause characteristics. Show students how word-by-word reading or inappropriate segmenting can be harmful to understanding (*the quick/ brown fox/ jumped/ over the/ lazy dog*). You can mark segments at first and then later allow students to divide text on their own. Segments can be lined up under one another like so:

EXAMPLE      Now is the time
for all good women
to come to the aid
of their gender.

or by slash lines in between:

EXAMPLE      Time/like the river/races some/
on downhill stretches/slowing
only/for the fight/with gravity.

Naturally, the second strategy is more like real reading, but the first is a good starting point for reading in units.

Put a dot at some central point of a meaning unit to aid students' focus and their intake of peripheral print. The size of the text unit to be viewed depends on readers' skills.

*EXAMPLE*

Once upon
•
a time
•
in a kingdom
•
by the sea
•
there lived
•
an awful truth
•

## SELF-IMPROVEMENT

Instruction in rate lends itself nicely to a whole unit in reading self-improvement. Since reading rates can be timed and charted, it is easy to see concrete progress. Students seem to enjoy this kind of intrapersonal and/or interpersonal competition. You need to stress to them, however, that rate increase with an accompanying comprehension decrease is undesirable.

Also, a gradual increase is recommended, so when students are tempted to hit #1 on the speed charts, caution them that minimal comprehension rates of 70 to 80 percent are required to chart the increase.

## FAST OR SLOW?

Urge students to take it slow on difficult material but speed up when the reading is easy. To motivate them, it may be necessary to show students that their current rate is uniform, no matter what the reading task. Time students in different reading situations that have varied purposes. You might want to time them first as they read for fun, and then as they study a textbook chapter. Together with students, calculate their words per minute:

$$\frac{\text{words in selection} \times 60}{\text{seconds}}$$

in each reading situation. Words per minute should be lower for the textbook chapter, but rate of comprehension for both studying and reading recreationally should be at least 70 percent.

## CUES

Knowing something about how writing is crafted is important for skimming and scanning, two essential fast-reading techniques. Knowing where main ideas are usually found and how to find signal words are two strategies that allow students to know when one idea is starting and the next beginning. When readers feel that they know enough about one idea, they can skip to the next.

Main ideas in nonfiction are often found in topic or concluding sentences, in boldface headings or subheadings. In fiction, main ideas are often inferred from the story title, theme, or moral.

In addition, there are many signal words to help readers. *More, also, and, therefore, consequently, finally,* and *in conclusion* tell readers that there will be another idea coming up or that they are nearing the end. *But, not, however,* and *rather* tell readers that a change of idea or point of view is coming up and that they need to pay closer attention.

## SKIMMING

Often students fear skimming because they believe they are missing something important when they skip words. To prove to them that they can get a wealth of information from skimming, xerox a selection and then blank out some of the words. Ask students to read the selection and then ask questions that can be answered by the information available in the text that still shows. Then ask other questions that tap on information hidden by the blanked-out spaces and ask students to make guesses. In some instances, you may need to convince students to be satisfied with comprehension scores that are less than perfect, but still acceptable (not less than 75%). Explain that skimming isn't a good idea in a study/test situation, since they are then aiming at "perfect" comprehension.

## SCANNING

Locating specific information within a text is simplified and speeded up for students who can scan. Show them how to move their index finger rapidly over lists or connected text in order to find the key word(s) for the information they need. The key words of a sentence are usually the noun and verb.

The use of practical sources such as phone books and dictionaries, and textbook features such as indexes and tables of contents, are ideal for beginning scanning instruction. In these sources, information is found in list form, and there is often a single key word, usually a noun. As students become better scanners, help them to transform questions about a text into partial statements and then scan for the answers. (How far did Susan run? Susan ran_____.)

## EYE SPAN

To help word-by-word readers, it is often necessary to increase their eye span for phrases. So the techniques listed under Reading in Idea Units are helpful here, too. We also recommend that students be shown that their eyes are actually taking in more than the word they are currently reading aloud. To demonstrate, slam (gently) the book a student is reading, and have the student finish the line of text aloud. Students are often amazed to find how effectively and efficiently their eyes and brain work together without intervention from their voice.

## Ssssh

There are a number of strategies for reducing lip reading or internal pronounciation during silent reading, thus ensuring a more rapid reading rate. A push for speed in a self-improvement program and an emphasis on reading in phrases are two strategies that have been discussed.

Two additional techniques focus on encouraging students to stop movements of the lips or throat because these features are otherwise engaged. In the first, students gently bite a finger, knuckle, pencil or popsicle stick, making lip and tongue movements difficult. The second has students stop internal pronunciation by mumbling numbers in order, saying a sound like "Z-Z-Z-Z," or even reciting a favorite song lyric or poem. Meanwhile, their eyes are moving over the words, attempting to process them through the eye-brain connection, instead of through the more accustomed eye-voice-brain chain.

With both techniques, students may at first experience some detachment from the words when they can't use their lips or throat. Comprehsion may suffer for a while, but it will soon pick up again.

# Activities to Go

NAME: **Get the Signal**

*SKILL:* The effect of signal words on reading speed

*MATERIALS:* Game board, 26 cards, a marker for each player

*PROCEDURE:*
1. The words and phrases listed below are printed on black cards. The pile of cards is turned face down in the center of the board.
2. Students choose cards in turn. They read the word or phrase and advance their markers according to the following:

If a "Full Speed Ahead" card is picked, move ahead 2 spaces.
If a "Go Ahead" card is picked, move ahead a space
If a "Slow" card is picked, do not move.
If a "U-Turn" card is picked, move back a space.

| FULL SPEED AHEAD | GO AHEAD | SLOW | U-TURN |
|---|---|---|---|
| and | thus | as a result | but |
| more | so | finally | yet |
| moreover | consequently | in conclusion | nevertheless |
| more than that | accordingly | at last | although |
| furthermore | | | however |
| also | | | still |
| likewise | | | otherwise |
| in addition | | | in spite of |

# GET THE SIGNAL

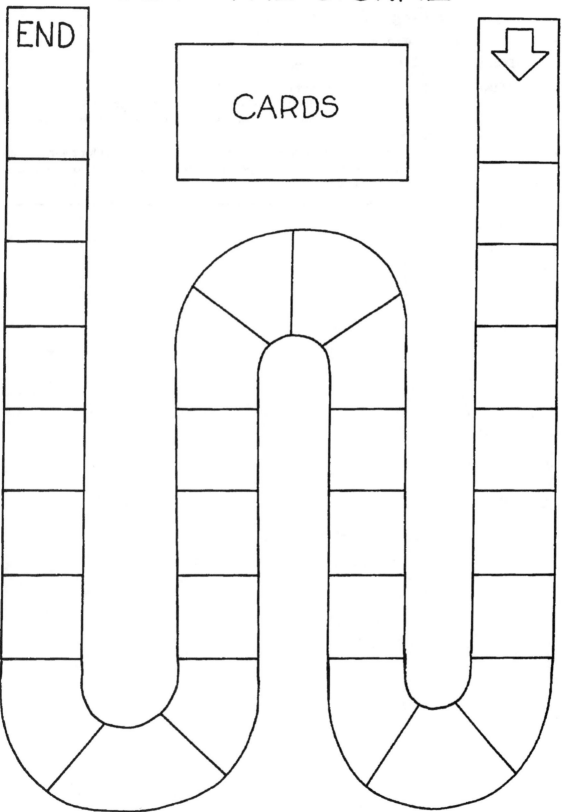

END

CARDS

NAME: **Reading Rate Record**

SKILL: Flexible reading rate

MATERIALS: Copies of the chart, file folders, pencils

PROCEDURE:
1. Make copies of the chart for your students.
2. Help your students fill out their copies at each rate improvement session.
3. Keep the charts in individual folders so that students can monitor their own progress.
4. Help students choose appropriate level and genre material for their purpose. The material should have accompanying comprehension questions, or you can write them yourself.

NAME:_____ DATE: _____

I.  **BEFORE READING**

Title _____ Author _____

Number of words _____ Genre _____

Purpose for reading (to get ready for a test, for fun, to get information, to get a general idea, to enjoy the words, other)

_____

_____

_____

What you already know about the title _____

_____

_____

Your expected reading pace (study, average, rapid, skim, scan) _____

_____

II.  **DURING READING**

Time yourself

Start:   Hour _____   Minutes _____   Seconds _____

Finish:  Hour _____   Minutes _____   Seconds _____

III. **AFTER READING**

1. Answer comprehension questions.

2. Compute comprehension score (% of questions answered correctly)

_____

3. Compute words per minute _____

**147**

# 13

# Motivation

## DESCRIBING THE SKILL

The best instruction in the world is wasted on students who aren't "there." Some of these students, openly hostile, disrupt the classroom. Others may appear attentive, but their glassy stares are an attempt to hide disinterest and daydreaming. Still others can't see how school learning relates to "real life." They may read dutifully in class, but never develop true interest in reading, thereby limiting their reading achievement and enjoyment.

Reading and language arts instruction usually receive the lion's share of classroom time in the elementary grades. But the amount of that allotted time in which students are engaged or attentive may be much, much less. This chapter deals with ways to increase engagement so that good instruction can have its effect.

## IDENTIFYING THE SKILL NEED

When children first get to school, they are usually quite excited about learning to read. They see it as a part of growing up and unlocking the print all around them. But for many students, their initial enthusiasm fades. This may be the result of one or several of the following factors:

- Reading disinterest may be the result of school experiences. Dull, routine reading instruction cannot compete with the razzle-dazzle of the media. You may believe that learning that arises from inner motivation is best and that students are not in school to be entertained. However, we must grab and hold students' attention if we are to teach them.
- Some children have so much trouble learning to read that for them reading is always a great effort and often a failure experience. Their rejection of reading is usually a defensive reaction. These students may very much want to read well and often, but may believe it impossible.
- At a certain stage of development, usually adolescence or even pre-adolescence, peer culture reflects (or does it dictate?) a rebellious, anti-authority stance. If adults say "read," then not reading becomes the thing to do. Social life and the screen culture (TV, movies, videos, computers) vie for students' attention and often win.
- Another reason for lack of motivation among some students may be the kinds of material that they encounter at certain times in their school careers. Some children in the lower grades, for example, are uninterested in the controlled

vocabulary stories that form their reading curriculum. They prefer the content of nonfiction on topics that are especially interesting to them. Conversely, some children in the upper grades may prefer the stories of the early grades or the recreational reading of paperback chapter books to the content area textbook reading now required of them.

- Last but not least are the students who are not paying attention because their reading instruction is not sufficiently challenging. You would expect that these students would be easy to identify, since they'd be acing every evaluation. But these "coasters" may not succeed to that degree—not because of ability, but because of inattention or complacency.

To find out why students may be having difficulty paying attention to reading instruction or may be unmotivated to read beyond school requirements, a group discussion or individual interviews can be effective. When leading an interview or discussion, keep the following suggestions in mind:

1. Use open-ended questions in order to let students do most of the talking.
2. Don't express negative judgments or attitudes about what students want or don't want to read.
3. Ask students to suggest ways to get and maintain their interest.
4. Don't ask questions about students' family reading or viewing habits.

## TEACHING THE SKILL: TECHNIQUES AND ACTIVITIES

The following additions and modifications for motivating reading are divided into those suited for (1) low-achieving readers, (2) average and above average readers, and (3) all students.

### LOW-ACHIEVING READERS

**Tender, Loving Care**
Students who don't do well in reading need a certain degree of special handling. It is necessary to acknowledge their learning difficulties without laying blame. Convince students that you can and very much want to help. Be honest, but immediately hatch a plot for change. Other evidence of tender, loving care:

- Take it easy with corrections. You or other students should do some correcting, but only after discussing the difference between mistakes that change text meaning and mistakes that don't. Remember to make only necessary corrections.
- Some students respond to a caring touch, a hand on their shoulder as they work. Sometimes just your nearness is enough. Get away from your desk and circulate to motivate.

**High Interest, Easy Vocabulary Materials**
These specially prepared books, workbooks, kits, and tapes are not for every student. But for those who accept these materials, they are worthwhile. First they can provide the independent-level readability that is essential to improved achievement. Second, they allow for successful completion, since most selections are short

and at a low conceptual level. Also these materials are frequently self-teaching so that individual instruction can occur.

### High-Interest, Challenging Vocabulary Materials

Sometimes employing frustration level reading material makes sense, especially when older students are insulted by easy texts. Recommended are trade magazines of interest to particular students. The usefulness of the articles, columns, and advertisements in these magazines depends on the amount of teacher direction provided. Vocabulary and concept development, guided reading, and student responses will make these materials instructional, not merely recreational in purpose. Of course, just skimming these magazines is fun, and should be allowed on occasion.

### Low-Interest, Easy-Vocabulary Materials

Sometimes students can be convinced that material written at their reading level, but below their age level is the best thing for them. This is especially true for very vulnerable students for whom mistakes are traumatic, and for true nonreaders of any age. In these cases, you must assure students that these very simple books will be replaced as soon as possible. Upper-grade students can be convinced to polish the oral reading of a low-level story in order to read it to younger children at home or in their school.

### Why Read?

Use functional materials with students. Newspapers, maps, menus, traffic and street signs, catalogues, game instructions, and advertising copy are just some of the text sources that inform people and help them make their way in the world. The use of these materials with reluctant readers is advised to show them that reading is useful, purposeful, and will increase their competence in their surroundings.

### Use of Kits, Games, and Self-Checking Material

Because skill levels are low with poor readers, it is essential to provide for skill practice. This is sometimes best accomplished through self-checked and paced work. Low-achieving students often feel bored or defensive when presented with teacher-directed lessons on topics they feel they should have mastered long ago. Individual work that is self-regulating allows for self-respect.

A teacher-made kit called a Lap Pack is especially effective for this kind of skill practice. (Lap Packs are so-called because they have everything an individual student needs to develop a skill, and it all fits in a folder or envelope that can rest on a lap!) You can focus on a needed skill and combine it with a student's interests. Lap packs can contain worksheets, games, reading selections, books, puzzles, and comic strips, among other materials—selected with a student's skill needs and interests in mind. When several students have the same need and interests, they can take turns having the lap pack and working through its contents.

### Use Brief, Frequently Changing Activities

Poor readers, like some preschoolers, have short attention spans. When the traditional academic period is forty minutes, schedule two or three reading/language arts activities for that time. Try to alternate active with passive actitivies, teacher-directed with independent ones, silent with oral reading, and skills with connected reading, to maintain attention.

## AVERAGE AND ABOVE-AVERAGE STUDENTS

### "Shock Therapy"

In general, average and high-achieving students have been lulled into confidence about their abilities in reading as well as in other subjects by the time they reach the middle grades. Just telling them and their parents that "things will be different in middle school (junior high, high school)" may have a minimal effect. Showing them how things are different is better.

To start, find a passage or story written at the students' instructional level. It should be complex in meaning. Raise higher level questions (inferential, critical, evaluative) about this material that you believe students will find difficult. Show how to "dig" for answers. Often this challenge will spark interest. You, then, are challenged to provide reading that will keep such students challenged!

### Old Techniques in Sheep's Clothing

For college-bound students, study skills are a must. But although many students have had such instruction before, the skills are yet unmastered. In order to get students' attention, it is often necessary to rework the standard techniques for teaching these skills.

1. One example is called "Harvard Outlining." Using the terms *sets* and *subsets* for main ideas and details, you can put a new status-conscious twist on outlining.
2. Use computers to stimulate interest in reading. The skill practice on much educational software is lackluster, but use of the hardware puts a new twist on the same old thing.
3. Another idea is to re-dress the standard book report. Instead of requiring a written report, substitute these book reactions:
   - *Use Drama*—Ask students to interview a character from the story, dramatize a favorite portion of a book, or arrange a story theater, in which one student reads aloud and the others pantomime the story action.
   - *Reread*—Have students revisit exciting sections of a book by reading them aloud to others. They may especially enjoy entertaining younger children with a polished reading of a favorite story.
   - *Book Recommendations*—Students enjoy rating the books they've read and sharing their opinions with peers. Once a book has a student's seal of approval, it's easier to "sell" to other students.
   - *Student-Teacher Conferences*—Ask students to summarize the story, or read or tell about their favorite/least favorite part. Keep your questions to a minimum so that students do most of the talking.

## TECHNIQUES FOR ALL STUDENTS

### Rewards

With some children, concrete rewards for reading accomplishments make sense. From stickers, to stars, to take-home paperbacks, you may find that tokens, along with praise, yield temporary motivation. Only intrinsic rewards, however, are permanently motivating.

### Oral and Choral Reading

• *By students*—Although oral reading has come under fire from many reading specialists because it leads to inappropriate silent reading habits and because it is frequently boring, in certain settings it can be used motivationally. Sometimes students beg to be allowed to read aloud. Perhaps oral reading maximizes comprehension for auditory learners. And finally, shared oral reading (choral reading) allows the better readers to support poorer ones.

To improve conditions for oral reading, help with unknown words should be quickly supplied, so there won't be long pauses as students struggle with words. To improve conditions for choral or shared reading, be sure every student can see the Big Book, or has access to the material being read.

*By teachers*—If you are a primary teacher, you probably already read to your students. If you teach the upper grades, you may not think it's necessary to read aloud, since your students can read more on their own. But for motivation, language and vocabulary development, and literary appreciation, there's nothing like reading aloud to your students. To maximize reading aloud time, teachers at all levels need to:

Choose something with obvious interest for your students.

Vary selections so that many types of literature are sampled.

Stop reading before students get bored.

Use your dramatic talents.

### Ready, Set, Read!

Teacher-directed instruction (vocabulary development, guided reading, student response), although necessary for developing skills, may not be the best way to engender interest. So save some time for students to read without instructional responsibility. This is usually called uninterrupted sustained silent reading (USSR) or sometimes independent reading.

### Use of "Sure-Fire" Books

Whether students read these independently or they are part of your instructional plan, these books have the approval of educators, librarians, and most importantly, kids. Of course the list could be longer, and not each child will love every book, but if you try these, you're bound to have some success. Sometimes certain characters are quite popular and there will be several books about them. Most of the books by the authors listed below are popular.

*Lower-Grade Choices*

Brett, Jan—*Berlioz the Bear*
Bridwell, Norman—the *Clifford* books
Brown, Marc—the *Arthur* books
Carle, Eric—*The Very Hungry Caterpillar*
dePaola, Tomie—*Strega Nona*
Lobel, Arnold—the *Frog and Toad* books
Martin, Bill, Jr.—*Brown Bear, Brown Bear*
Numeroff, Laura—*If You Give a Mouse a Cookie*
Parish, Peggy—the *Amelia Bedelia* books
Rey, H. A.—the *Curious George* books
Sendak, Maurice—*Where the Wild Things Are*
Seuss, Dr.—*Green Eggs and Ham*
Wood, Audrey—*The Napping House*

*Middle-Grade Choices*

Banks, Lynne R.—*The Indian in the Cupboard* (trilogy)
Blume, Judy—the *Super Fudge* books
Cherry, Lynne—*The Great Kapok Tree*
Cleary, Beverly—the *Ramona* books
Cole, Joanna—the *Magic School Bus* books
Dahl, Roald—*The BFG*
Fritz, Jean—*George Washington's Breakfast*
MacLachlan, Patricia—*Sarah, Plain and Tall*
Pinkwater, Daniel—*Fat Men from Space*
Scieszka, Jon—*The True Story of the Three Little Pigs*
Steig, William—*Amos and Boris*
Van Allsberg, Chris—*Jumanji*
Warner, Gertrude—the *Boxcar Children* books
White, E.B.—*Charlotte's Web*

*Upper-Grade Choices*

Gardiner, John R.—*Stone Fox*
George, Jean—*My Side of the Mountain*
Juster, Norton—*The Phantom Tollbooth*
Lowry, Lois—*Number the Stars*, the *Anastasia* books
Naylor, Phyllis Reynolds—*Shiloh*
Paterson, Katherine—*Bridge to Terabithia*
Paulsen, Gary—*Hatchet*
Rawls, Wilson—*Where the Red Fern Grows*
Spinelli, Jerry—*Maniac Magee*
Soto, Gary—*Pacific Crossing*
Taylor, Mildred—*Roll of Thunder, Hear My Cry*

**Media Links**

The connections between TV, movies, and the publishing world is well known. Students respond to the advertising that accompanies new releases. Therefore, they may be quite interested in the "novelized" scripts. Comparing the book and the movie is a good way for students to discover the strengths of the print medium. They often find that their image of characters and setting is superior or at least more personal and satisying than those depicted in the visual media.

**That's Me!**

Sometimes, as luck will have it, students will find themselves and their life situations in books. The "shock of recognition" that occurs when book meets boy (or girl) can change a student's relationship to literature. This kind of meeting is hard to arrange, but worth a try.

Some blind dates do work! It's a matter of knowing students and literature well enough to be a good matchmaker.

# ■ *Activities to Go*

NAME: **Rate-a-Read**

SKILL: Instructional vocabulary

MATERIALS: Rating sheet

PROCEDURE: After finishing a story or book, a student completes the rating sheet below. Both the numbers 1 to 5 and smiling/frowning faces are offered so that students have a choice of response style. Writing space is provided after each response set, in case students want to explain or elaborate.

VARIATION: When students read nonfiction, the statements below may be substituted for those on the rating sheet.

1. This book (article, chapter) was so interesting, I could hardly put it down.
2. The author knows a lot about his/her subject.
3. I know something about this subject, but I found out even more.
4. This was the first time I'd read about this subject, and now I'd like to read more about it.
5. The author explained things well.
6. The author had facts to back up his/her opinions.
7. I liked the writing style.
8. I'd read another book by this author.
9. I'd read another book on this subject.
10. I'd recommend this book to a friend.

# RATE-A-READ RATING SHEET

After reading each sentence on the left, circle a number or face that shows your opinion about your book or story. One (or the big smile) means that you agree quite a bit. Five (or the big frown) means you disagree quite a bit. The other three numbers and faces are less strong opinions. If you wish, you may explain your rating on the "Why do you think so?" line.

1. This book (or story) was so exciting I could hardly put it down.
   *Why Do You Think So?* _____

2. I learned something about myself from this book.
   *Why Do You Think So?* _____

3. I was able to imagine places described in this book.
   *Why Do You Think So?* _____

4. The author used language clearly.

   *Why Do You Think So?* _____

5. The author used language beautifully.

   *Why Do You Think So?* _____

6. The characters were interesting people. I'd like to know more about them.
   *Why Do You Think So?* _____

7. I know some things I never knew before.

   *Why Do You Think So?* _____

8. I like the author's sense of humor.

   *Why Do You Think So?* _____

9. I'd like to read another book by this writer.

   *Why Do You Think So?* _____

10. I'd recommend this book to a friend.

    *Why Do You Think So?* _____

NAME: **Video Snack**

SKILL: Motivation

MATERIALS: Game board shown in Figure 13.3

PROCEDURE: 1. The "snacks" are left blank on the game board so you can print the words that match students' interests. The words below would be useful for students who enjoy video games. Other high-interest lists are found in the "Variations" section.

*Video Game Vocabulary*

| | |
|---|---|
| strategy | simulation |
| graphics | technique |
| controller | tactics |
| cartridge | version |
| system | customize |
| details | joy stick |
| arcade | split screen |
| gear | virtual reality |
| web | net |

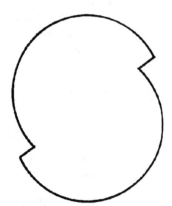

2. Students using the "S" cut-out as a game piece, attempt to eat all the snacks (identify all the words) located along the paths they take to get through the maze. The object is to get from start to finish following a single path. When players encounter an unknown word, they begin again, trying another path. Once a path has been mastered, students can try another path, or attempt to increase their speed of word identifications on the mastered path.

VARIATIONS: *Car Vocabulary*

| | |
|---|---|
| clutch | registration |
| radiator | transmission |
| battery | fender bender |
| accelerator | Sunday driver |
| downshift | V-8 engine |
| windshield | defroster |

*Sports Vocabulary*

| | |
|---|---|
| touchdown | inning |
| face-off | relay |
| tackle | marathon |
| strikeout | slam dunk |
| foul ball | volley |

# VIDEO SNACK

FINISH

START

# 14

## Standard English
## as a Second Dialect

### DESCRIBING THE SKILL

Everyone speaks a dialect. A dialect is a language variation that has special phonological, synactical, and semantic qualities. Dialects formed because of closely knit regional and social groupings. Because certain regions or social classes have greater prestige, so do certain dialects.

Such is the case with standard English, the dialect of the majority of people living in the United States. use of nonstandard English, the dialect of many African-Americans, for example, can stigmatize speakers. Since standard English is the dialect of the mainstream, and of the institutions of the majority, reading teachers may believe that the ability to speak standard English is necessary for success in learning to read.

Other educators have challenged that assumption. First, because speech is an important part of personal identity, changing or adapting it is often disagreeable and difficult. Second, there is research that shows that speaking nonstandard English need not interfere with comprehension of written standard English. But it may (1) limit students' horizons, (2) hamper student-teacher communication, (3) give a distorted view of students' oral reading ability, and (4) occasionally interfere with comprehension.

### IDENTIFYING THE SKILL NEED

To find out if students' nonstandard dialect is interfering with their oral reading and their reading comprehension is a multistep process. First it is helpful to know how much nonstandard English is part of students' speech and which features of the dialect they use. This information is important when evaluating oral reading and reading comprehension.

To identify students as either standard or nonstandard speakers is difficult for a couple of reasons. One is that people can change their language to fit varied social settings. Shy children, for instance, may speak nonstandard English, but respond in school in monosyllables that are hard to evaluate. Other students may be able to speak standard English, but refuse to do so because of peer-group pressure. Another reason is that there are ranges of dialect usage among individuals.

Some students speak "a lot" of nonstandard English while others use few features infrequently.

To find out if students are having oral reading or reading comprehension problems because of their nonstandard dialect, however, is somewhat easier. Effective oral reading is always done for an audience. If students who speak nonstandard dialect have had an opportunity to practice to the point of comfort and confidence the text they will read aloud, and if their audience is receptive and accepting, success is probable. So speaking nonstandard English need not interfere with oral reading performance. To discover whether students' oral reading comprehension is affected by their nonstandard dialect, two kinds of evaluations are helpful. The first requires an examination of nonstandard dialect speakers' oral reading miscues. If there is a miscue pattern evident, such as the omission of *-ed* or *-s,* you might ask students questions about the text that deal directly with tense and number. When students answer such questions incorrectly, evidently using their misreadings as a guide, you can assume their speech pattern is interfering with oral reading comprehension.

To check for interference in silent reading, you can ask nonstandard dialect speakers comprehension questions that directly address some of the features you know to be a part of their language. If certain students usually omit the possessive marker's, be sure to ask them questions about what belongs to whom, when the opportunity arises in a story discussion. Similarly, when your students use double negatives in their speech, you may want to direct questions about what did or did not happen in a particular text.

## TEACHING THE SKILL: TECHNIQUES AND ACTIVITIES

### ACCEPT NONSTANDARD ENGLISH DURING ORAL READING

To accept nonstandard English means that you need to know its features so that you can distinguish between dialect miscues and reading miscues when students read aloud. Acceptance of your students' nonstandard language helps them to build self-esteem. It also sends this message: "Helping you to understand what you read is the major purpose of reading lessons." The following compares written standard English (SE) with spoken nonstandard English (NSE).

| | | | EXAMPLES | |
| *Category* | *Feature* | *Explanation* | *Written SE* | *Spoken NSE* |
|---|---|---|---|---|
| Phonological | Final consonant cluster simplification | Words ending in a consonant cluster have the final letter of the cluster absent | *desk* | "des" |
| | *th* sounds | initial voiced *th* pronounced as /d/ | *that* | "dat" |
| | | medial and final voiceless *th* pronounced as /f/ | *bathroom* | "bafroom" |

*(Cont.)*

| Category | Feature | Explanation | EXAMPLES Written SE | Spoken NSE |
|----------|---------|-------------|---------------------|------------|
| | | medial and final voiced *th* pronounced as /v/ | *mother* | "muhver" |
| | | final *th* in *with* pronounced /d/ or /t/ | *with* | "wid" "wit" |
| | final consonant devoicing or absence | voiced stops /b/, /d/, and /g/ are pronounced like corresponding voiceless stops /p/, /t/, and /k/ | *fed* *pig* | "fet" "pick" |
| | | loss of final consonant sounds | *mad* | "ma" |
| | absence of medial consonants | medial consonants can be omitted | *little* *help* *worry* *throw* | "lil" "hep" "wo'y" "thow" |
| | effect of nasal consonant | the /g/ in *ing* is absent | *running* | "runnin" |
| | | use of a nasalized vowel instead of the nasal consonants | *balloon* *rum* | "balloo" or "balloom" "ru" or "run" |
| | | short vowels *i* and *e* do not contrast | *pin* and *pen* | "pin" |
| | *str*- cluster | *str*- clusters are pronounced /skr/ | *street* | "skreet" |
| | long *i* | long *i* is pronounced like the *a* in *father* | *time* | "tahm" |
| | article *an* | the article *a* is used whether the following word begins with a vowel or a consonant | *an umbrella* | "a umbrella" |
| | verb forms with *to* | when following a verb, *to* is pronounced "ta" or "a" | *have to* *went to* *going to* | "hafta" "went a" "gonna" |
| | stress patterns | stress is placed on first syllable on some words which have second syllable stress in SE | *gorilla* | "gó-ril-la" |
| | | first syllable can be absent when it is unstressed | *about* | "bout" |
| | final *t* followed by *'s* | when final *t* is followed by the *'s* of a contraction, the *t* is not pronounced | *it's* *what's* | "is" "whas" |
| | *ask* | for the word *ask*, the final consonant cluster is reversed | *ask* | "aks" |

*(Cont.)*

| Category | Feature | Explanation | EXAMPLES | |
|----------|---------|-------------|----------|---|
| | | | *Written SE* | *Spoken NSE* |
| | consonant *v* | *v* is pronounced with a sound which is unknown in SE—it sounds somewhat like /b/ or /w/ | *over* | "ober" "ower" |
| | *don't* | this word can lose its initial sound as well as its final sound | *don't* | "on" |
| Morpho-logical | loss of *-ed* suffix | the past tense marker *-ed* is absent | *missed* | "miss" |
| | the present tense suffix | the present tense marker *-s* used for the third person singular is absent | *he wants* | "he want" |
| | plurals | the plural marker *-s* is absent | *toys* | "toy" |
| | possessives | the possessive marker *'s* is absent | *boy's* | "boy" |
| Syntactical | irregular past tense | irregular past tense forms are replaced by present tense forms | *said* | "say" |
| | the past participle | with irregular verbs, the past tense and the past participle may interchange | *he has come* | "he has came" |
| | | | *he has taken it* | "he taken it" |
| | the verb *to be* | the verb forms *is* and *was* are used for all persons and numbers | *they're running* | "they's runnin' " |
| | | the verb forms of *to be* are often missing | *she is tired* *they're busy* | "she tired" "they busy" |
| | invariant *be* | *be* is used as a main verb, regardless of person and number | *sometimes he is busy* | "sometime he be busy" |
| | auxiliary deletions | auxiliary verb forms are absent | *he is going to school* *she'll have to go home* | "he goin'a school" "she have to go home" |
| | negation | more than one negative marker | *he doesn't know anything* | "he 'on' know nothin' " |
| | relative clauses | in relative clauses, relative pronouns can be absent | *that's the dog that bit me* | "tha's the dog bit me" |
| | | in relative clauses, *what* can replace relative pronoun | | "tha's the dog wha' bit me" |
| | question inversion | indirect questions follow direct question rules | *his mother asked why he was late.* | "his mother was he late" |
| | | direct questions follow indirect question rules | *why did he take it?* | "why he did take it?" |

*(Cont.)*

| Category | Feature | Explanation | EXAMPLES Written SE | Spoken NSE |
|---|---|---|---|---|
| | *there* constructions | existential *there* is replaced by *it* | *there was a convertible outside* | "it was a convertible outside" |
| | pronominal apposition | a noun and its pronoun are the subject of a sentence | *his mother threw out the balloon* | "his mother, she th'ew out the balloo' " |
| | use of *at* after *where* | questions that begin with *where* end with *at* | *where is she?* | "where she at?" |
| | undifferentiated pronouns | SE nominative forms of personal pronouns are used to show possession | *that's his book* | "tha's he book" |
| | reflexives | pronouns formed with the possessive form of the personal pronoun plus *self* | *himself* | "hisself" |
| | demonstratives | the use of *them* when SE requires *those* | *I want some of those candies* | "I want some a them candies" |

## ALLOW STUDENTS TO SEE NONSTANDARD DIALECT IN PRINT

This technique will allow nonstandard-English-speaking students to build self-esteem through language pride and demonstrate to them the link between speech and print. It also allows standard-English-speaking students the opportunity to build respect for another dialect of their language.

### Trade Books That Include Nonstandard English
What follows is a list of some well-known and some recently published library books that include nonstandard English, usually in the dialogue.

Clifton, Lucille, *Three Wishes*, Dell, 1994.
Johnson, Angela, *Tell Me a Story, Mama*, Orchard, 1992
McKissick, Patricia, *Flossie and the Fox*, Dial, 1986
Reschka, Chris, *Yo? Yes!*, Orchard, 1993
Steptoe, John, *Stevie*, Harper, 1986

### Use the Language Experience Approach
You may wish to employ nonstandard English when students make their own reading material. You will probably want to copy the students' syntactic patterns and word choices. Phonological features, however, should not be incorporated into spellings (i.e., "fahn" for *fine;* "runnin' for *running*). The reasons? They make the story more difficult to decode. Such spellings, too, have negative literary and historical associations for many African Americans.

## HELP STUDENTS TO ACQUIRE STANDARD ENGLISH

Although the block of time allotted to teaching the language arts is already "crowded," it makes sense to use part of it for giving help to students who need to acquire standard English. Standard English instruction and reading instruction, however, should not be intermingled. Otherwise, students may confuse the goals of speaking with those of reading. It is also important not to delay instruction in reading until standard English is acquired, since it may be years before a second dialect is mastered.

Remember that informal opportunities for standard English already exist, particularly if you have a mixture of dialects in the school and community. Television provides access to standard English, but live language models have greater impact. Most importantly, you can be a model of standard English. Read aloud to nonstandard English speakers (and all others, too!) everyday. This will give them the opportunity to hear standard English at length instead of in conversational or instructional snatches.

Before formal instruction in standard English begins, explain dialect differences to students. Emphasize the functions of school versus home languages. Be sure students understand that they are not being asked to give up their primary dialect.

Use parallel, contrasting structures as your primary instructional technique. Several activities for this kind of teaching follow.

### Hear the Difference
Read pairs of sentences that contrast standard with nonstandard features to students and have them identify the difference(s).

*EXAMPLES*

| They are pin pals. | He miss the bus. | When it rain, he got a úmbrella. |
| They are pen pals. | He missed the bus. | When it rains, he has an umbrélla. |

### See the Difference
Show pairs of sentences that contrast standard with nonstandard English to students and help them to point out the differences.

*EXAMPLES*

| I ain't got none. | He be my best friend. | She wonder why was he late. |
| I don't have any. | He is my best friend. | She wondered why he was late. |

### Call and Response
Give students a standard English phrase or sentence. Have them respond with the nonstandard equivalent. Then reverse roles and give the dialect phrase or sentence and ask students to give the standard English. At a later point, some students may be ready to be callers.

*EXAMPLES*

| *Call* | *Response* |
| --- | --- |
| He hasn't any sisters or brothers. | He ain't got no sister or brother. |
| Fred loves all of his pets. | Fred love he pet. |
| Once upon a time there lived a girl named Cinderella. | One time it was a girl. She name Cinderella. |

### Make a Dictionary, Use a Dictionary
The semantic features, or vocabulary, of nonstandard English were omitted from the list of dialect features, because they change frequently. Just when standard English speakers think they have a handle on nonstandard vocabulary, it changes,

making adults who think they are hip look silly! The best source of current jargon is your students.

Ask them to make their own nonstandard dictionary, if they wish. You may also want to consult some published dictionaries of or texts about nonstandard English to enhance your teaching. An up-to-the-minute source is *Black Talk* by Geneva Smitherman (Houghton, 1994).

# Activities to Go

*NAME:* **Match-a-Meaning**

*SKILL:* Matching standard and nonstandard English words, phrases, and sentences

*MATERIALS:* Game board; word, phrase, and sentence lists

*PROCEDURE:* 1. Photocopy the number of gameboards you will need for players.
2. Print standard words, phrases, and sentences in appropriate boxes. Be sure each player's card has these in a different order.
3. Play like BINGO. The caller reads the nonstandard words. Players must cover with a marker the box that contains the equivalent nonstandard expression. Five across, down, or on the diagonal wins.

*Sample Words:*

*Nonstandard*—aks, boaf, ain't, mas', hisself, wait, pólice, got, brothers
*Standard*—ask, both, isn't, mask, himself, waited, police, have, African American males

*Sample Phrases:*

*Nonstandard*—be busy, the house what Jack built, runnin' a Joe, he short, Carla say, the hawk, hit you upside you head, messin' wid, main man, run it by me
*Standard*—is busy, the house that Jack built, running to Joe, his shirt, Carla said, windy cold weather, smack you in the head, harrassing, best friend, explain it

*Sample Sentences:*

*Nonstandard*-It was a garbage can on the sidewalk. Where Henry at? Judy, she be the teacher. They laughin'.
*Standard*—There was a garbage can on the sidewalk. Where's Henry? Judy is the teacher. They're laughing.

*VARIATIONS:* Synonyms

*Words:*

a. dine, fall, chubby, mind, trip, start, trunk, road, stone, smart
b. eat, autumn, fat, listen, voyage, begin, suitcase, highway, pebble, brainy

*Phrases:*

a. very thin, chocolate bar, clothing, writing tools, cereal box, uncle, cup and saucer, father, in a minute, to the grocery
b. skinny, candy, pants and shirt, pen and pencil, breakfast food container, mother's brother, dishes, male parent, very soon, to the store

*Sentences:*

a. The robin sang a joyful song. Water splashed on my good shoes. Mom sent me to the store for a loaf of bread. I'll take the train to town.
b. The robin sang a merry tune. My good shoes were splashed with water. Mother sent me for bread. I will take the subway downtown.

# MATCH-A-MEANING

| WORD | PHRASE | SENTENCE | PHRASE | WORD |
|------|--------|----------|--------|------|
| | | | | |
| | | | | |
| | | MATCH – A-MEANING | | |
| | | | | |
| | | | | |

# Who Knows Where or When?

SKILL: Morphemes that signal tense or possession

MATERIALS: Game board and sentences with questions below

PROCEDURE: Choose these sentences or create your own. Write them or read them aloud. The example shows how answers are placed on the game board.

EXAMPLE  We danced at Jack's house.

   a.  Where was the dancing? jackhouse, Jack's, school
   b.  When was the dancing? now, yesterday, later
       "Jack's" is placed on the board in the house.
       "yesterday" is placed on the board in the clock

1.  Joan will slip three boxes into Lee's shopping bag.
    a.  Where is Joan slipping three boxes?
        *in a shop      into Lee      into Lee's bag*
    b.  When is Joan putting boxes in a bag?
        *now      later      before*
2.  I jog four times around Darron's block.
    a.  Where do I jog?
        *around my house      near Darron's house      four times*
    b.  When am I jogging?
        *last week      next month      each day*
3.  They were swimming in Kevin's pool when it began to thunder.
    a.  Where did they swim?
        *in a boy's pool      in thunder      at Kevin's*
    b.  When did they swim?
        *in the past      in the present      in the future*
4.  Frank says "This is my sister Laverne's house. Let's visit."
    a.  Where does Frank visit?
        *at his sister's      at my sister's      at Laverne's office*
    b.  When is Frank visiting?
        *this day      two weeks ago      in the fall*
5.  The telephone rang three times before it was answered at the Johnson's.
    a.  Where is the phone call?
        *at John's      at the Johnson home      at John's son's home*
    b.  When is the phone call?
        *three times      several days ago      tomorrow*
6.  Last week Bob pushe6•d Fran across Kelly's lawn in the baby carriage.
    a.  Where did Bob push Fran?
        *into a baby carriage      across Kelly      on Kelly's lawn*
    b.  When was Bob pushing Fran?
        *some time ago      this afternoon      on Saturday*
7.  She will take a trip to her grandmother's farm.
    a.  Where is she going on her trip?
        *to grandmother's      to mother's farm      to a grand farm*
    b.  When is the trip?
        *this July      some time in the future      last Christmas*

8. Five girls will present the play "Thanksgiving Memory" in Ms. Carol's class.
   a. Where is the play?
      *in the classroom*      *at Carol's*      *in the carol room*
   b. When is the play?
      *soon*      *before*      *on Halloween*

*VARIATIONS:* Literal comprehension: Compose sentences that contain both "when" and "where" information. Have students write "where" information in a house and "when" information in a clock. "Who" and "why" information from sentences you create may be inserted into large drawings of a person and a question mark, respectively.

# WHO KNOWS WHERE OR WHEN?

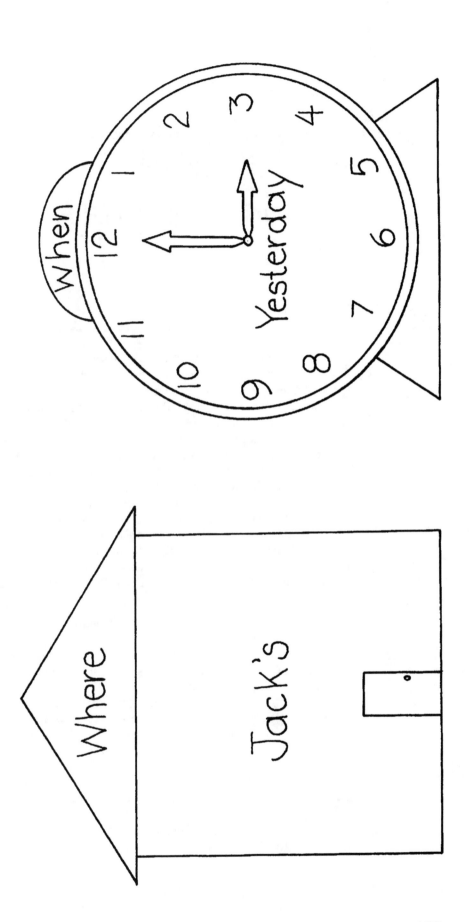

169

# 15

# English as a Second Language

## DESCRIBING THE SKILL

Reading is a language-based activity. When second language learners begin to read in English, certain difficulties can arise. This chapter will discuss some of those special issues and make suggestions to cope with them.

Although there are many other first languages currently represented in our schools (Vietnamese, Chinese, Haitian speakers of French, Russian, and Navaho are examples), Spanish will be the only one considered in this chapter because (1) Hispanic students represent the vast majority of non–English speakers in the United States, and (2) focus on a specific language allows for a pointed discussion and a more practical chapter. However, it is expected that teachers of other second language students can apply the suggestions in this chapter to their situations.

It should be noted that language differences exist among groups of Spanish speakers. Mexican-Americans, Puerto Ricans, and Argentinians, for instance, use differing dialects of Spanish. Culturally, too, each of these groups is unique, a fact to consider when selecting interest-based reading materials.

There are three groups of Spanish speakers who are learning to read English. They are:

a. *Preliterate*—Students who are literate in neither language because they haven't yet been taught to read.
b. *Literate in Spanish*—Students who are literate in their first language because of bilingual instruction in the States, Spanish instruction in another country, or reading instruction at home.
c. *Functional illiterates in both languages*—Students who have failed to learn to read in either language in one or a variety of settings. For them, limited oral proficiency in one or both languages is also characteristic.

## IDENTIFYING THE SKILL NEED

There are two major reasons why reading instruction needs modification when second language learners are concerned. The first involves a lack of sufficient En-

---

* The authors wish to thank Angela Malovich Castro of English Language Trainers, Newburyport, Massachusetts for her guidance in the writing of this chapter.

glish vocabulary. This lack will affect both decoding and reading comprehension. For second language learners, oral language programs should both precede and accompany reading programs, whenever possible.

A second issue that concerns teaching reading to second language learners arises because of differences between students' first languages and English. Because of these differences, second langugage learners may have difficulties reading English. Phonics ability and oral reading performance can be affected. Grammatical and conceptual problems may lead to comprehension difficulties.

The following table highlights key phonetic and grammatical differences between Spanish and English. Knowledge of these potential points of interference can help teachers anticipate students' difficulties and plan appropriate instruction. It is important to note that not all listed features are characteristic of all Spanish dialects nor of the speech of every individual who speaks Spanish as a first language.

| Category | Feature | Explanation | English | Possible Interference |
|---|---|---|---|---|
| Phonological | /i/ = /e/ | Short *i* is pronounced as long *e*. | *sin* <br> *ship* | "seen" <br> "sheep" |
| | /e/ = /i/ | Long *e* is pronounced as short *i*. | *sleep* | "slip" |
| | /a/ = /e/ | Long *a* is pronounced as short *e*. | *late* <br> *sale* | "let" <br> "sell" |
| | /v/ = /b/ | /v/ and /b/ are represented by only one sound in Spanish, which is close to the sound /b/. | *very* <br> *vote* <br> *valentine* | "bury" <br> "boat" <br> "Ballentine" |
| | /ch/ = /sh/ | The Spanish pronunciation of /ch/ sounds like /sh/. And sometimes /sh/ sounds like /ch/. | *much* <br> *teacher* <br> *ship* | "mush" <br> "tee-shir(t)" <br> "chip" |
| | /th/ | Initial voiced /th/ is pronounced as /d/ and final unvoiced /th/ is pronounced /s/. | *this* <br> *bath* | "dis" <br> "bass" |
| | /j/ = /y/ <br> or /ch/ <br> /y/ = /j/ | J is pronounced as /y/ or /ch /, while initial *y* is pronounced in an approximation of /j/. | *job* <br><br> *just* <br><br> *yes* | "yob" or <br> "chob" <br> "yust" or <br> "chust" <br> "Jess" |
| | Absence of final consonants | Because /p/, /t /, /k/, and /f/ do not appear in the final position in Spanish words, these sounds are often omitted from English words. This is particularly true with multisyllabic words or words in phrases. | *hate* <br> *economic* <br> *student* <br> *get off* <br> *climb up* | "hay" <br> "economy" <br> "studen" <br> "get o' " <br> "climb u' " |
| | Final consonant cluster simplification | Spanish has no final consonant clusters so there is pronunciation difficulty with final clusters | *cats* <br><br> *hopped* <br> *moved* | "cat" or <br> "cass" <br> "hop" <br> "move" or <br> "mood" |
| | Initial *s* clusters | Spanish has no initial consonant beginning with /s/. There is a tendency for Spanish speakers to make a syllable out of an /s/ blend by adding /e/ to its beginning. | *sleep* <br> *smile* <br> *skin* | "esleep" <br> "esmile" <br> "eskin" |

*(Cont.)*

| Category | Feature | Explanation | English | Possible Interference |
|----------|---------|-------------|---------|----------------------|
| Morpho-logical | Superlatives | In English, comparative adjectives are inflected (large, larger, largest). In Spanish, other comparative adjectives and articles are added to the first (grande, más grande, el más grande). | *larger* *largest* | "more large" "more larger" or "the more large" |
| | Possessive | There is no possessive case form in Spanish. "John's hat" is "El sombrero de Juan." This causes comprehension problems only infrequently. | *John's hat* *the mother's cat* | "The hat of John" "John hat" "the mother cat" |
| | Stress | In Spanish, an accent mark over a letter shows that the syllable in which that letter occurs is stressed. Otherwise, the stress usually falls on the last syllable, unless that syllable ends in an *n, s,* or a vowel. In those cases, the second syllable gets the stress. In English, the first syllable of a root is stressed. | *comment* *pilot* *language* *tortoises* | "commént" "pilót" "langúage" "tortóises" |
| Syntactic | Future tense | In Spanish, the most common future tense employs an inflected verb. In English "will" is the most common future marker. Consequently, "will" is often omitted and unless the sentence refers to the future in some other way (i.e., "tomorrow"), comprehension problems may result. | *She will laugh.* | "She laugh." |
| | Pronouns | Spanish direct and indirect object pronouns come before the verb. English sentences with these features may be disordered by second language learners. Strings of two or more pronouns often cause big problems for these students. | *He showed it to me.* | "He showed me it." "He show me." "To me he show it." |
| | | The Spanish word "su" means "his," "her," and "your." So there may be some confusion among these words. Also, there is occasionally confusion among these possessive pronouns and subject pronouns. | *Mary showed her mother the flower.* | "Mary showed his mother the flower." "Mary showed she mother the flower." |
| | Negation | In Spanish a double negative is usual. (*"No tiene nada"* = "he has nothing") When reading English, where only one negative marker is used, comprehension may be affected. After reading *He has nothing* and being asked "Does he have anything?" the second language learner may reply, "Yes," since the negative was not emphatic enough. | *He has nothing.* | "He no has nothing." |

# TEACHING THE SKILLS: TECHNIQUES AND ACTIVITIES

Because oral language development is so important for second language learners, many of the techniques that follow focus on oral input from the students. But it should be noted that although oral language is practiced, pronunciation problems may not necessarily disappear with training. The oral language activities that follow serve best as a way to develop syntactic and semantic ability in spoken English and as a vehicle for growth in reading and writing.

## TALK AND TALK SOME MORE

Informal warm-ups and building background activities for lessons as well as more formal dialogues that are lessons in themselves are appropriate for second language learners. For example, pictures are excellent conversation stimuli. You can clip magazine photographs, use comic strips, or use prepared instructional visuals to motivate discussion or prompt stories. Sets of interrelated pictures that form a story can be helpful. Both *People Are Funny: Pictures for Practice* (Longman, 1987) and *Picture It* (Prentice, 1981) are recommended materials.

You may want to ask questions about these picture stories that can elicit the use of key problematic features in English. For example, if students need practice with the future tense of verbs, ask questions requiring students to predict outcomes. Detailed instructions for using picture stories for second language development can be found in the Activities to Go section at the end of this chapter (Get Talking).

## LANGUAGE EXPERIENCE APPROACHES

Using students' orally dictated sentences and stories as a basis for their reading material is a mainstay of second language instruction. After problem areas in speaking, reading, or writing have been identified, a list of observed points of interference can form some goals for instruction. For example, if a group of middle-grade children are substituting /b/ for /v/, they need speaking, writing, and reading opportunities to contrast /b/ with /v/. To provide such an opportunity, b and v words can be generated around a theme. The theme for a language experience unit might be "The Best Vocation for Me." Examples of key words for discussions, dictated stories, reading experiences, and follow-up activities are:

| | | |
|---|---|---|
| veterinarian | butcher | Boy Scout Leader |
| volunteer | baker | Vice-President |
| ventriloquist | Brownie leader | babysitter |
| barber | boss | |

In another case, you may wish to combine problem areas. If /b/ is substituted for /v/, /i/ for /e/, conditional markers omitted, and comparative adjectives confused, "Vampire Bats" could provide the theme! The key words would be:

| | | |
|---|---|---|
| bitten | sleep | bloody |
| bite | bleed | bloodier |
| biting | blood vessel | bloodiest |

## POINTS OF DIFFERENCE

Provide direct instruction for points of linguistic interference. Perhaps the most important graphophonic difference between Spanish and English is the amount of sound-spelling regularity. In Spanish there are twenty-seven letters and twenty-four sounds, while English has twenty-six letters and forty-three sounds!

Second language learners need an explanation of irregularities in the rules of phonics, and much practice applying the rules flexibly. Instruction in comprehending details may also be necessary with these students. Recommended are prereading discussions concerning time (tense), ownership of objects and relationships among characters (possession), negative attitudes and actions (John did/did not want to go), and pronoun references (Who is the "he"mentioned in the second sentence?), among other things. Postreading questions should also assess these areas.

## I'VE GOT RHYTHM

Help students with pitch, stress, and juncture. These terms refer respectively to the highness and lowness of words within contexts, the emphasis on syllables or words within sentences, and the pauses within and at the ends of sentences. Taken together, pitch, stress, and juncture give a language its unique rhythm. Instruction in language rhythm is rare, but valuable. In some instances, halting, awkward reading and inadequate reading comprehension may be improved. Some ways to help with English-language rhythm follow.

## ORAL READING

Literature written to be performed (plays), or read aloud for its sound qualities (poems), as well as fiction with an abundance of dialogue is suitable. You or other proficient oral readers in your class can provide models of expressive, rhythmic oral reading. You may also want to use prepared audiotapes of literature and have second language learners follow along in the accompanying books.

## SILENT READING

To help second language learners transfer the rhythms of oral language to silent reading, a series of marked passages is useful. This is done by underlining, indicating stress, and elaborating on punctuation through the use of color or size markings. An example of marked passages for silent reading can be found in the Activities to Go section of this chapter (Reading with Oomph).

## USE OF MUSIC

Folk songs with multiple verses are particularly effective, since students can learn orally the rhythm of the first verse, and apply it to a silent reading of the other verses. Collections of such songs are found in:

Glazer, Tom, *New Treasury of Folk Songs*, Bantam, 1978
Langstaff, Nancy and John, *Sally Go Round the Moon*, Revels, 1986.
Raffi, *The Raffi Singable Songbook*, Crown, 1980.
Seeger, Ruth C., *American Folk Songs for Children*, Doubleday, 1980.
Seeger, Ruth C., *Animal Folk Songs for Children*, Shoe String, 1992.

## CHANTS

Another way to highlight the rhythm and intonation patterns of English is through chants. Chants can set everyday situational English to the musical rhythms jazz, rap, rock, or blues. Carolyn Graham is an author of several collections of chants. Some of her books include:

*Big Chants: As I Went Walking*, Oxford University Press, 1991.
*Jazz Chants for Children*, Oxford University Press, 1978.
*Small Talk*, Oxford University Press, 1986.

## DEVELOP VOCABULARIES

Naturally, the biggest challenge faced by second language learners is vocabulary acquisition. All of our suggestions in Chapter 6 are relevant here. Other techniques especially aimed at the unique needs of second language learners follow.

### BEGIN WITH SPANISH BORROWINGS AND SPANISH-ENGLISH COGNATES

Because Spanish and English have a common ancestry (Latin) and mingled histories, a study of borrowings and cognates is profitable as well as motivating. (Borrowings are, at first, the same in spelling and meaning, but may shift over time. *Fútbol* in Spanish was borrowed from the English *football*, but the spelling changed to match the Spanish pronounciation. Cognates are the same in meaning, but may be slightly different in spelling. False cognates seem to be from the same source of meaning, but are deceptive. (*Embarazada* in Spanish means pregnant, not embarrassed!)

Here are some examples of Spanish borrowings. Note that all of the words are not common in all regions and cultures within the United States.

| | | |
|---|---|---|
| adios | coyote | poncho |
| adobe | fiesta | rodeo |
| barbeque | guitar | siesta |
| burro | macho | tacos |
| canyon | patio | |

Now for a brief list of cognates. Any Spanish-English dictionary will provide many more.

| | |
|---|---|
| alfabeto = alphabet | pantalones = pants |
| crayola = crayon | sabado = Saturday |
| julio = July | sinfonia = symphony |

### DEMONSTRATE WORD MEANINGS

When students' English is limited, it is difficult to define unknown words for them, because the meanings of the explanatory words or synonyms may also be unknown. For example, explaining the word hammer is a challenge when students don't know nails, strike, tool, wood, or build. A picture of a hammer, though of temporary use, is not sufficiently language-rich for large scale vocabulary acquisition. Demonstrating or pantomiming the driving of a nail into the wall makes meaning acquisition easier, especially if you explain simultaneously and then have students follow your lead. The pairing of language and action is particularly effective as a multisensory learning tool.

### EXPAND CONCEPTUAL NETWORKS

Second language learners are frequently culturally as well as linguistically different. Even when they have learned *yard*, for example, their image of a yard may be quite different from the one in a story. Eliciting the students' experiences with a word and then contrasting it with its meaning in a story helps to expand the students' schema by linking what they know with what they don't. One way to do this is by contrasting semantic webs, diagrams that illustrate word relationships. A web for yard might look like this:

## STUDENT'S IMAGE

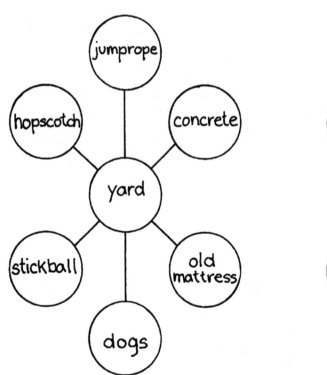

## STORY IMAGE

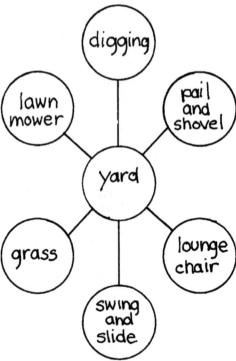

### PROVIDE INSTRUCTION FOR FIGURATIVE AND IDIOMATIC LANGUAGE

Nonliteral meanings are among the most difficult for second language learners to acquire. With idioms and figures of speech, the parts do not add up to the whole and a dictionary is of little help. Often students don't know that they don't know, since the literal meaning of a figure of speech or idiom may seem accessible, but unsuited for the context in which it's found. In these cases, comprehension problems are inevitable.

You need to anticipate the problems second language learners will have with the figurative and idiomatic language in a story and prepare students before they begin to read it. Direct skills instruction with idioms and figures of speech is also recommended. Students seem to love creating drawings of both the literal and figurative meanings of an expression.

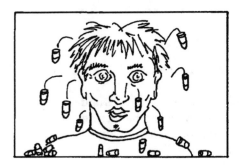 

And are there funnier books than the *Amelia Bedelia* series by Peggy Parrish for observing the "hazards" of misunderstood figurative language ?

Some recommended books for you and your students about the origins and explanations for figures of speech are:

Funk, Charles, *A Hog on Ice and Other Curious Expressions,* Harper, 1985.
Funk, Charles, *Heavens to Betsy! and Other Curious Sayings,* Harper, 1986.
Terban, Marvin, *It Figures! Fun Figures of Speech,* Clarion, 1993.

Books that help with idioms include:

Arena, John, *Idiom's Delight,* High Noon, 1991.
Dixon, Robert, *Essential Idioms In English,* Prentice, 1984.
Terban, Marvin, *Punching the Clock: Funny Action Idioms,* Houghton, 1990.

# Activities to Go

NAME: **Get Talking**

SKILL: Oral language development

MATERIALS: Story illustrations

PROCEDURE:
- Students ask questions about each picture. Answer them with only *yes* or *no*, according to the story you have created to go with the pictures.

EXAMPLE

Picture 1. Is that a stray dog?
Picture 2. Are those kids mean?
Picture 4. Are the children scared that their dog ran away?

- After students have exhauted their questions and know all about the pictures, have them put together a story, using the pictures to help with sequencing. A sample story for the illustrations below follows:
  1. A boy and girl are playing with a dog. They are throwing a stick and their dog is jumping for it.
  2. A group of bigger kids are putting together a kind of cart. They have one dog tied onto it, but they need another dog to tie to the empty rope.
  3. The first dog runs away and finds the tied-up dog. They're having fun playing together.
  4. The boy and girl are looking for their dog. The girl looks in a big box. The boy calls for the missing dog, whose name is Chico.
  5. The bigger kids start to tie up Chico.
  6. But the boy and girl find Chico. Will the bigger kids give him back? Will Chico want to stay with his new dog friend, or go back with the boy and girl?

VARIATIONS:
- Have students make up the story and you ask them questions.
- Use other kinds of materials, such as discarded basal readers cut up into word-less stories; wordless picture books, wordless comic strips, student-made sets of pictures.

**Reading with Oomph**

Pitch, stress, and juncture

MATERIALS: The marked narrative song below, or other printed matter that you have marked. (Choose poems or song lyrics that have dialogue and rhythm.)

PROCEDURE: The song below is to be read aloud by students, who can use the following key to interpret the markings.

1. Underlined once—say it softly.
2. Underlined twice—say it in a regular voice.
3. Underlined three times—say it loud.

Oh will you wear red

Oh my dear, oh my dear

Oh will you wear red, Jennie Jenkins

I won't wear red

I'll wear my jeans instead

I'll buy me a foll-de-roll-de

Till-de-toll-de seek a double

Roll Jennie Jenkins roll

Oh will you wear yellow

Oh my dear, oh my dear

Oh will you wear yellow, Jennie Jenkins

I won't wear yellow

'Cause I'm not a bowl of jello

I'll buy me a foll-de-roll-de

Till-de-toll-de seek a double

Roll Jennie Jenkins roll

VARIATIONS: 1. Put in stress marks, which mean "give this syllable emphasis." These may be added to or used instead of underlining.
2. Encourage students to really emphasize punctuation marks, by printing them extra large or extra dark.

# Appendix
# To Help Children Test Well

From the time children first enter school, you test them to find out what they know, how well they have learned, and what needs to be taught or retaught. You use a variety of testing situations and instruments, some of which are standardized. Standardized testing formats, however, may bear little or no resemblance to any instructions students have met in their daily classroom work. When trying to demonstrate knowledge of a skill under these circumstances, students must first try to figure out what they are being asked to do, and they may fail to follow the directions correctly. The difficulty that they experience with the testing format is sometimes incorrectly interpreted as a problem with the reading skill task rather than with the procedure.

Testing is anxiety producing, for most students, no matter how much you try to sugarcoat the procedure with elaborate explanations and rationalizations. The factors of timed tests and IBM answer sheets automatically produce stiffened backs. The jury is still out on the role anxiety plays in achievement. For some students, a little anxiety enhances performance, while for others it has detrimental results. In any case, *panic* is harmful.

We hope you will find the suggestions below helpful in your attempts to allay anxiety and thereby increase the validity of the test scores and diagnostic information you obtain.

## FAMILIARITY BREEDS SUCCESS

Familiarize students with testing format so they may concentrate on the skill being tested. Find out what testing instruments are used by your school or school system. Be sure to use the testing format (not the test items) in your daily work with students. The following example is a format commonly used.

*EXAMPLE*   Put your finger on the clown at the left.

R     R     R     S     R

Look at the letters to the right of the clown. Circle all of the letters that are the same. This procedure may be teacher-led or used with a tape and worksheet. The picture of the clown is used solely as a place marker. Its irrelevance to the task itself can be confusing.

## TEST WHAT YOU TEACH

If you are using a beginning approach with students that focuses on one aspect of the reading process (phonics, word patterns, sight words), do all you can to obtain a testing instrument that also focuses on that aspect. Students who have spent six months learning to read through a whole-language approach will not perform well at this point on a test that is better suited to those who have learned to read using short vowel patterns (*bad, beg, dim, run,* etc.).

## "HURRY UP; DON'T WASTE TIME"

For timed tests, teach students that when they are responding to paragraphs with comprehension questions, the following hints are helpful:

1. Read the questions first and then read the *whole* paragraph, underlining important points so that you can refer back quickly to specific information.
2. Answer the questions you know, skipping those you must mull over. (Be sure they circle each number they skip on the answer sheet. This not only helps students mark the answer sheet correctly, but also facilitates their returning to difficult items later in the testing.) When students have completed the first run-through of the test, they may return to those items which will require more thought. Spending too much time on an early item can prevent students from showing what they know before time runs out.

## TO LOSE ONE'S PLACE IS ONLY HUMAN

Losing your place on an IBM answer sheet when an item has been skipped or omitted is a problem most students encounter in their school careers.
Teach students to:

1. Circle or underline correct answers in the test booklet if this allowed, as well as on the answer sheet in case they need to go back and correct an answer sheet.
2. Circle the number of the omitted item on the answer sheet to highlight those questions unanswered.

*EXAMPLE*

3. With each item, make sure the question and the answer sheet numbers match before marking an answer.

You may also wish to make up worksheets for class exercises and use IBM answer sheets to give students practice.

## HELP!

Encourage students to ask for help if they encounter a procedure problem. Demonstrate that help will be given promptly and gladly. Provide assistance to students before panic sets in.

## WHEN TO GUESS

Test publishers often try to take into account the guessing factor by subtracting more for wrong answers than for omitted items. As teachers, you want to encourage educated guesses. If students have no idea as to what the answer is, they should go on to the next question and leave the unknown item blank. If however, they can narrow the choice to two answers, it is worth taking the chance and selecting one. Emphasize, however, that when only one answer is requested, only one may be marked.

# Index